The Gift of God

Richard A. Seymour

Integrity Press | LaGrange, WY

THE GIFT OF GOD
second edition
published by Integrity Press

ISBN 978-0-9760620-2-8

Printed in the United States of America

For information:
INTEGRITY PRESS
PO BOX 10
LAGRANGE, WY 82221

OTHER BOOKS BY RICHARD A. SEYMOUR
All About Repentance
Fishing For Men
Religion: Who Needs It?
The Gift

Dedicated to Hix
and the memory of a man named Dot.

CONTENTS

The Gift

Have you ever been loved unconditionally? Have you ever been accepted just as you are by others, without any need to improve your image first? Are you aware that God's love for you is personal and absolutely unconditional, and that He will accept you as you are? There are no impossible rules or conditions for you to keep before He will love you. There are no fees—no need or demand for you to pay for God's favor. There are no religious hoops you must jump through to gain His mercy; nothing you must join before you can enjoy His lovingkindness. You don't have to attempt to impress Him, for He already knows all about you, and loves you anyway.

For nineteen years of my life I knew little or nothing of God's love for me. My idea was that God loved only good boys, but not bad boys like me. Imagine my surprise when I found out God, the Creator of the universe, had a personal love for me. The most convincing way God has proved that love for me, as well as for all people, is by offering us the greatest gift ever known. He offers it to us freely; it can be ours simply by receiving it.

This book is written with everyday people in mind—some who have never darkened the door of any church, temple or synagogue. My purpose is to share with you the great news of this gift, a truth expressed so beautifully in this well known Bible verse—John 3:16: "For God so loved the world that He gave His only begotten Son, that whoever believes in Him should not perish but have everlasting life."

Learning that God loves me in a personal way has made such a difference in my life. I also want you to know this great love and the gift He offers to you.

The Gift of Eternal Life

Many have no idea that the greatest gift this world has ever been offered is absolutely free and lasts forever. We'll talk about what the gift is, how to obtain and have it forever, and what it means to be born into God's family.

From the very outset I want you to be aware of God's love for you and of His provision for you to have the gift He offers—eternal salvation. I want you to understand that God loves you. Contrary to what you may think, God loves the world—yes, the world of sinners. The Word of God makes this abundantly clear.

> But God demonstrates His own love toward us, in that while we were still sinners, Christ died for us.
>
> Romans 5:8

For God so loved the world that He gave His only begotten Son, that whoever believes in Him should not perish but have everlasting life.

John 3:16

This is a faithful saying and worthy of all acceptance, that Christ Jesus came into the world to save sinners, of whom I am chief.

1 Timothy 1:15

God's unconditional love for mankind is a gift—it is freely bestowed. There is nothing you can do to cause God to love you, because He already does. No amount of good works, no effort on your part, no generous or meritorious endeavors of your own, no determination or promise to do better in the future—*nothing* causes God to love you. He just does. That's the way He is.

You may be under the impression that God hates the sinner, but as we have seen from the Bible, this is not true. It is true, however, that God hates sin—so much so that no sin will be allowed to dwell with God forever. God makes it clear that nothing sinful will dwell in His new Heaven. Consider these verses:

But there shall by no means enter it anything that defiles, or causes an abomination or a lie, but only those who are written in the Lamb's Book of Life.

Revelation 21:27

> For You are not a God who takes pleasure in wickedness, nor shall evil dwell with You.
>
> Psalm 5:4

There is a seeming paradox in God's Word. On the one hand, God loves the sinner and wants him in Heaven; on the other hand, to go to Heaven man must be perfect, which he is not. Obviously there are some people who are better than others from a comparative standpoint, but in the eyes of God we all come short of His perfection.

> As it is written, "There is none righteous, no, not one."
>
> Romans 3:10

> For all have sinned and fall short of the glory [perfection] of God.
>
> Romans 3:23

> All we like sheep have gone astray; we have turned, every one, to his own way; and the LORD has laid on Him the iniquity of us all.
>
> Isaiah 53:6

> For there is not a just man on earth who does good and does not sin.
>
> Ecclesiastes 7:20

These verses express that all people do wrong things. In Ecclesiastes 7 we see that even good ("just") people still sin.

The answer to the paradox is the very heart of the real

Gospel. Here's what I mean: The religious world—even among so-called Christians—teaches that if you are good you will be saved or go to Heaven, and if you are bad you will go to hell. Well, I'm sure you'll agree that no matter how good you may be, you are not perfect, any more than I am. It isn't goodness that is required for entrance into Heaven, it's perfection! If we determined to live a perfect life from now on—and if we had the power to do it—we would still need a Savior because of the sins we had already committed. If nothing else, past sins in our lives disqualify us for entrance into a perfect Heaven.

If we have to be perfect to go to Heaven—and remember, none of us are—then it would be foolish to talk about getting there by our own good works. No amount of good works could make us perfect. If we are ever going to receive this perfection it would have to be given to us; there is no way to earn, merit or achieve it. In fact, this is exactly what the Bible says.

> For by grace you have been saved through faith, and that not of yourselves; it is the gift of God, not of works, lest anyone should boast.
>
> Ephesians 2:8–9

> Not by works of righteousness which we have done, but according to His mercy He saved us.
>
> Titus 3:5

> For the wages of sin is death, but the gift of God is eternal life in Christ Jesus our Lord.
>
> Romans 6:23

> And I give them eternal life, and they shall never perish; neither shall anyone snatch them out of My hand.
>
> John 10:28

A gift is a voluntary transfer of something of value without anything provided in return. It is unearned by the recipient, and received without cost or obligation. A gift is complete only when it has been received by the recipient; otherwise it is just an offer that has been ignored or refused. A gift is to be received. The giver may pay for or create the gift, but the one for whom the gift is intended can do nothing but receive it.

Now what do we have so far?

1. *Perfection is required for entrance into Heaven.*

2. *None of us are perfect.*

3. *We cannot earn, work for or merit this required perfection.*

4. *It must be God's free gift to us.*

God's One Condition

The important question at this point is, "How does one receive this gift of eternal life?" At least 150 times in the New Testament God declares that the one condition for receiving eternal life, or salvation, is belief in Christ.[1] Notice how clear some of these verses are:

> Most assuredly, I say to you, he who believes in Me has everlasting life.
>
> John 6:47

> He who believes in Him is not condemned: but he who does not believe is condemned already, because he has not believed in the name of the only begotten Son of God.
>
> John 3:18

> Most assuredly, I say to you, He who hears My word and believes in him who sent Me, has everlasting life, and shall not come into judgment; but has passed from death into life.
>
> John 5:24

> But these are written, that you may believe that Jesus is the Christ, the Son of God, and that believing you may have life in his name.
>
> John 20:31

> These things I have written to you who believe in the name of the Son of God; that you may know that you have eternal life, and that

you may continue to believe in the name of the Son of God.

1 John 5:13

Since believing in Christ is the only condition for salvation according to God's Word, it is important to know what the Bible means by "believe." If I asked you if you believe in George Washington, you would naturally say, "Yes." What would I mean by the question? I would mean, do you believe that he lived, and that he was the first President of the United States of America—in other words, the historical facts about him. But then, if I asked you if you believe in your parents, your answer may be yes or no, because by asking this question I would mean do you *trust* your parents—do you have faith in them. The same word believe is used in both questions, but with different meanings. The Biblical word believe is a word that means to trust in, rely upon, or to depend upon. When God says, "Believe on the Lord Jesus Christ and you shall be saved," He does not mean to just believe that Christ existed. Neither does He mean for us to only believe certain doctrines about Christ, such as: He was born of a virgin, He was God in the flesh, He died for the sins of the world, and He's coming again. Believing about Christ is one thing; believing in Him is another. To believe in Him is to trust Him alone for our salvation; it is to depend upon Him to get us to Heaven; it is to have faith in Him, that He will do what He promised to do—give us eternal life.

We see, then, that although we are sinful and cannot obtain eternal life by working for it, we can receive this eternal life as a gift from God, through faith in Christ. You see, Christ is none other than God Himself in human form who came to earth to pay for man's sin. The Bible puts it this way:

> For the Son of man has come to seek and to save that which was lost.
> Luke 19:10

> For God did not send His Son into the world to condemn the world, but that the world through Him might be saved.
> John 3:17

> Who Himself bore our sins in His own body on the tree, that we, having died to sins, might live for righteousness—by whose stripes you were healed.
> 1 Peter 2:24

> For Christ also suffered once for sins, the just for the unjust, that he might bring us to God, being put to death in the flesh, but made alive by the Spirit.
> 1 Peter 3:18

The following verse is one of the clearest verses on this point. It tells us not only what happened when Christ died, but also what we receive when we trust Him.

> For He made Him who knew no sin to be sin for us, that we might become the righteousness of God in Him.
>
> 2 Corinthians 5:21

If those who believe in Christ receive God's righteousness through faith in Christ (see Romans 4:5), then nothing can add to or improve upon that. God's righteousness is His perfection received by faith in Christ. If someone tells me that in addition to having faith in Christ I must also join the church, give money, or be baptized to be certain of my salvation, I want to know one thing: "What can joining the church, giving money, or water baptism add to God's righteousness?" You cannot improve upon "the righteousness of God." You see, my being good before I believed in Christ could not save me; neither can being good after I believe in Christ save me, or help keep me saved. Once a person receives the gift of God's righteousness (which is why we can live forever), there is nothing in the whole wide world that can add anything to that. What a great gift of salvation God provides!

The New Birth

Perhaps you have heard the term "you must be born again." What is the new birth? How can you know whether you have been born again? What does it mean to be "a child of God?" We turn to the Bible, God's Word, to find the answers to these questions and many more.

Jesus told Nicodemus in the third chapter of John that a man must be "born again" to enter or even see the Kingdom of God. The Savior explained to this devoted religious leader that just as a person is born of the flesh he must also be born of the Spirit from above.

In John 1:12–13 we are told how this new birth comes about: "But as many as received Him, to them He gave the right to become children of God, to those who believe in His name: who were born, not of blood, nor of the will of the flesh, nor of the will of man, but of God." As a matter of fact, Jesus makes the new birth imperative. He said, "You *must* be born again" (John 3:7).

Many say they believe that to be saved or to go to Heaven one must be born again. However, those who believe that a saved person can lose his salvation, believe in the new birth only as a doctrine, not as a miraculous reality. But when a person trusts Jesus Christ as Savior he is actually born into God's family; he becomes His child in reality—not just in theory. God does, in fact, become His Heavenly Father. This is not just an opinion or doctrine to agree with, but, for the true believer in Christ, it is a most precious reality. I cannot emphasize this strongly enough.

The new birth is a miracle. The new birth is not necessarily a feeling, or an experience, or an "encounter." For one trusting Christ, it is a fact. When I trusted Jesus Christ as my Savior, I was at that moment born into God's family. In my own case, I was disappointed because I experienced no special feelings. I had always been told that "if you ever get saved, boy, you'll feel it"—but I didn't. Nevertheless, based on God's infallible Word, I had the promise of eternal life: "Most assuredly, I say to you, he who believes in Me has everlasting life" (John 6:47). At the moment I believed, I was born into God's family and became a child of God.

In James 1:18 God says a person is born again of His will and by His Word. "Of His own will He brought us forth by the word of truth." Also, in 1 Peter 1:23 it says, "Having been born again, not of corruptible seed but of incorruptible, through the Word of God which lives and abides forever." Feelings may or may not accompany the birth, but feelings certainly are neither the cause nor necessarily the evidence of the new birth.

When we believe in Christ we are born into God's family; we become His children with all the rights and privileges of His family; and He becomes our Father with all the rights and privileges of a father. As our Heavenly Father, He is able to take care of His children. Unlike earthly fathers, God is the perfect Father. He cares for us, teaches us, and disciplines us, all in the best ways possible. He is working in our hearts. If His child is obedient, He blesses him; and whether His child is obedient or disobedient, He trains or disciplines him.

The new birth is simply what happens when one receives Christ as their Savior. It is God becoming our Heavenly Father upon our belief in Christ.

Knowing the gift of God is eternal life is one thing; having that gift as your very own is something else again. Let's consider the importance of receiving this gift from God.

Receiving This Gift

It's wonderful to be offered a gift, especially when the gift is eternal life from God. You know that "the gift of God is eternal life through Jesus Christ our Lord." Now is the time to receive it. The last phrase of 2 Corinthians 6:2 says, "Behold, now is the accepted time; behold, now is the day of salvation." In addition, Hebrews 2:3 warns, "How shall we escape if we neglect so great a salvation." It's safe to assume that God never promises to save anyone tomorrow or at a more convenient time, and that's simply because we just do not know if we'll even be alive tomorrow! God further warns of our human tendency to procrastinate. Notice how clear Proverbs 27:1 is: "Do not boast of tomorrow, for you do not know what a day may bring forth." Today is the time to receive God's gift of eternal life through faith in Christ. We have no guarantee of any time other than right now. So, let's talk about how to receive this gift.

As stated in Chapter One, a gift must be received for it to benefit the one for whom it is intended. God wants you to receive His gift of eternal salvation, be with Him forever, and have a personal relationship with Him. Here is the way He expresses it:

> For this is good and acceptable in the sight of God our Savior, who
> desires all men to be saved and to come to the knowledge of the
> truth.
>
> 1 Timothy 2:3–4

The "all men" whom God desires to save certainly includes you, doesn't it? You may feel unworthy of such love and concern, and truly you are—as are all of us. You may have little self-respect or feel no self-worth whatever. Perhaps you feel so worthless and unloved that you have even contemplated suicide. But regardless what your opinion is of yourself, God's opinion is what matters, and He desires to save you forever. You are that important to Him.

It is essential to realize that just because God wants all to be saved, and offers salvation as a free gift to all, does not mean anyone is automatically saved and on the way to Heaven. The gift of eternal life must be received. And just how do you do that? The answer is provided in John 1:10–12:

> He [Christ] was in the world, and the world was made through
> Him, and the world did not know Him [the greatest oversight in all
> of history!] He came to His own, and His own did not receive Him.
> But as many as received Him, to them He gave the right to become
> children of God, to those who believe in His name.

You "receive" Christ as your Savior by "believing on His name." What is His name and what does it mean? Before

Jesus' birth an angel appeared to encourage Joseph to take Mary as his wife, explaining that she was still a virgin and that her conception was of the Holy Spirit. Part of the angel's explanation included this revealing statement regarding Christ's birth:

> And she will bring forth a Son, and you shall call His name Jesus, for He will save His people from their sins.
>
> Matthew 1:21

The name Jesus means "God who saves" or "God saves" or "God's salvation." To "believe in His name" (John 1:12) means you believe that He is who and what His name implies— God who will save you. To believe in Christ literally means you trust Him, you rely upon Him, you depend upon Him, you count on Him to do what He promised—to give you everlasting life, to save you, to make you His child, to forgive you.

Immediately after Christ's birth another angel appeared to shepherds and said to them:

> Do not be afraid, for behold, I bring you good tidings of great joy which will be to all people. For there is born to you this day in the city of David a Savior, who is Christ the Lord.
>
> Luke 2:10–11

"Good news...great joy...to all people...a Savior!" Can you

think of any reason why you should not trust in such a wonderful Savior? Do you trust in Him now to save you? If you do, why not thank Him for dying on the Cross for you, for rising from the dead, and for offering you the free gift of salvation? Though prayer is optional, you may want to express your faith and your gratitude to God for such a great salvation something like this: "Thank You, Lord, for sending Your Son to die in my place for my sins, and for conquering death through His resurrection. I now trust in Christ alone for my eternal salvation, and look forward to my new life as Your child. In Jesus' name, Amen." Whether you pray a prayer or not, the one thing that makes salvation yours is faith in Christ alone. This is stated so simply and beautifully in Romans 4:5:

> But to him who does not work but believes on Him who justifies [declares righteous] the ungodly, his faith is accounted for righteousness.

Remember it is a gift, offered apart from any attempts on your part to earn it or work for it. What amazing grace!

In summarizing these first two chapters it might be helpful to present the truths covered in a simple outline form that you may easily grasp. I remind you that the word Gospel means "good news," as explained in 1 Corinthians 15:3–4, where the apostle Paul described the Gospel as follows: "For I delivered to you first of all that which I also received: that Christ died for our sins according to the Scriptures, and that He was buried, and that He rose again the third day according to the Scriptures." Christ's sacrificial death on Calvary as payment for our sins and His conquering of death through His resurrection are the absolute necessary components of God's saving message. Without His death and resurrection there would be no salvation to offer. Here, then, is that wonderful Gospel story in a nutshell.

God's Demand

Man must be perfect—as perfect as God—to qualify for Heaven.[2]

God's demand is that man must be perfect, but only God is perfect. No human—other than the God-man, Jesus—is or ever has been perfect. Yet that is the requirement for entrance into God's perfect Heaven. Psalm 5:4 says, "For You are not a God who takes pleasure in wickedness, nor shall evil dwell with You."

Man's Condition

Man is not—nor can he be—perfect, because he has already sinned.[3]

Nothing is as untrustworthy as man's wicked and deceitful heart, so we dare not trust in our feelings, hunches or impressions. To do so would be placing our faith in what God considers the most unreliable source—our deceitful heart. God's Word describes man's heart this way in Jeremiah 17:9: "The heart is deceitful above all things, and desperately [incurably] wicked; who can know it?"

God also describes man's best behavior as filthy rags in Isaiah 64:6: "But we are all like an unclean thing, and all our righteousnesses are like filthy rags; we all fade as a leaf, and our iniquities, like the wind, have taken us away." If all of our "righteousnesses"—the *best* we can produce—are like filthy rags in God's sight, what must our average or worst behavior seem to Him? If our very best efforts fall far short of His perfection, then without His intervention there is no hope for any of us.

God's judgment or penalty for sin is death (separation).[4]
Biblically speaking, all people without Christ are already spiritually dead or separated from God (Ephesians 2:1). When we die physically, our soul and spirit are separated from our body, and physical death is one appointment we will never be late for or miss. Hebrews 9:27–28 states: "And as it is appointed for men to die once, but after this the judgment, so Christ was offered once to bear the sins of many."

In addition, those who die in unbelief, are eternally separated from God. This final separation is hell, and is the ultimate "wages" of sin (Romans 6:23).

Man can do nothing of himself to obtain this perfection.[5]

We see clearly from God's Word that sinful, imperfect man cannot earn or merit eternal life by anything that he is or by anything that he does. That's why so many Bible passages emphasize that salvation is "not by works" and only comes to the believing sinner through faith and by God's grace, and in no other way.

An honest person will have to confess, "If perfection is demanded by God for me to go to Heaven, then obviously I do not qualify." Such an accurate but painful realization leads us to ask the question, "Then how can I go to Heaven?"

God's Provision

He sent His Son, the Lord Jesus Christ, to be our Savior, our Sin-Bearer. Christ paid the penalty of our sin for us and rose from the dead, thus proving the debt had been paid and accepted by the Father.[5]

God Himself has made provision for us to know Him, have a personal relationship with Him, and one day live with Him in Heaven. There was no other possible way for God to provide eternal salvation for man other than through sending His Son to die in our place, because Galatians 3:21 states: "For if there had been a law [or principle] given which could have given life, truly righteousness would have been by the law."

With sin's debt paid, salvation is offered freely to man as the gift of God.[6]

Romans 3:21–23 reveals that the one who places his faith in Christ is declared righteous before God, and verse 24 explains that the believer is "justified freely [without cost] by His grace through the redemption that is in Christ Jesus." To be "justified freely by His grace" means that grace is free—it cannot be earned or bought by any of man's efforts or intentions. This is why some of us speak of "free grace" when referring to salvation. By definition grace is free, but since Scripture itself emphasizes the freeness of grace it is important for us also to emphasize this point. Many religious people would say that salvation is by God's grace and still think they have to work to gain their salvation. They simply do not understand the true freeness of God's great eternal salvation.

Man's Response

Man must personally believe in the Lord Jesus Christ to obtain this gift of salvation.[7]

When you put your trust in the Lord Jesus Christ it is not the same thing as having faith that He will see you through your surgery, nor is it trusting Him to work out a problem of some kind. To "believe" means to rely upon, to trust in Him or believe in Him for what He has promised—eternal life. That's what He came to provide for those who do believe in Him. The Biblical response from the unbeliever can be summed up in the phrase: By grace alone, through faith alone in Christ alone—nothing more, nothing less, and nothing else!

God's Guarantee

The true believer in Christ may be certain of his or her salvation now, in the present, and once salvation is received it can never be lost.[8]

It is not uncommon for the Christian to have doubts at times, especially during those moments or days when we are not following the Lord faithfully. We begin to look within ourselves and pose such questions as, "Could I be truly saved and think these thoughts or do these things?" An important habit to develop is to always base your confidence in Christ and His Word alone, never in yourself or in what others may think about you. Someone once put it this way: "I may tremble upon The Rock, but The Rock never trembles under me!" We change; God does not. What He has promised He is also able to perform—and He will (Romans 4:20–21). Since God Himself says that the one who places his or her faith in Christ is saved forever, that settles it. How we might feel about it at any given time does not change what our Faithful God has guaranteed. Thank the Lord this is true!

You may want to jot down the main points of this outline to have a simple reminder of how to share the Gospel.

God's Demand: Perfection
Revelation 21:27; Psalm 5:4; Habakkuk 1:13

Man's Condition: Unperfect and Sinful
Romans 3:23; Isaiah 64:6

God's Provision: His Son and Salvation by Grace
John 3:16; Ephesians 2:8–9

Man's Response: Believe on the Lord Jesus Christ
John 3:18; Romans 4:5

God's Guarantee: Eternal Life
John 5:24, 6:47; 1 John 5:13

The message is so simple that most people stumble over it thinking that "it just can't be that easy." God has indeed made salvation easy for us, and simple to understand, because He doesn't want anyone to miss it or to fail to grasp the wonderful message of the Gospel. God has done the hard part. He has made the one sacrifice that can take away sin and provide eternal life for mankind. Once we comprehend what He has done for us, how can we possibly not believe in the Lord Jesus Christ? Common sense dictates that only a fool would pass up such a totally awesome and wonderfully satisfying gift!

If you have now received Christ as your Savior there are many wonderful promises that God makes to you as His child. As you read His Word you will begin to learn so much about Him. The next four chapters are devoted to important areas that will greatly benefit you as a new believer.

The Holy Spirit

Jesus promised that after He went back to His Father in Heaven, the Holy Spirit would come to live within all true believers in Christ. The Holy Spirit is the believer's guarantee, as well as our Power, Guide, and Instructor. Once we place our faith in Christ, His Spirit dwells with us and in us forever—He is our guarantee of eternal life.

Every believer in Christ is not only placed into God's family (the new birth), but is also indwelt by the Holy Spirit. Jesus said:

> If anyone thirsts, let him come to Me, and drink. He who believes in Me, as the Scripture has said, out of his heart will flow rivers of living water. But this He spoke concerning the Spirit, whom those believing in Him would receive.
>
> John 7:38–39

One of the ways God assures us we are His is by sealing us with His Spirit. This great promise is expressed in Ephesians 1:13–14:

> In Him you also trusted, after you heard the word of truth, the gospel of your salvation; in whom also, having believed, you were

sealed with the Holy Spirit of promise, who is the guarantee of our inheritance.

The believer is sealed in Christ by God the Father through the Holy Spirit. Second Corinthians 1:22 puts it this way: "God who also has sealed us and given us the Spirit in our hearts as a guarantee." The Holy Spirit gives evidence or proof of our belonging to Christ and is the pledge of our inheritance which will reach completion when we see the Lord face to face.

A second reason God gives us the Holy Spirit is that His Spirit empowers us to live as God wants us to. We now have the power within to develop Christlike characteristics in our day-to-day lives. God's desire for His children is that they be used as "instruments of righteousness," not letting sin be in control but rather yielding to the Spirit's control (see Romans 6:12–13). Galatians 5:16 puts it this way: "Walk in the Spirit and you shall not fulfill the lusts of the flesh."

Walking in the Spirit is simply choosing to live in God's truth. The Holy Spirit is our Guide and Instructor into this truth. As we study God's Word the Spirit will lead us into truth as John 16:13 says: "When He, the Spirit of truth, has come, He will guide you into all truth." Also, in 1 Corinthians 2:12 it says: "Now we have received, not the spirit of the world, but the Spirit who is from God, that we might know the things that have been freely given to us by God."

Can I Lose the Holy Spirit?

The Holy Spirit's relationship to God's children has differed at times. This has caused some to misunderstand the teaching of the Holy Spirit and His relationship to believers today. In the Old Testament the Holy Spirit would often "come upon" various men in order to perform a particular task. When that task was accomplished He would leave them. His coming and going had to do with their service, not their salvation. For instance, in Psalm 51 David prayed, "Do not take Your Holy Spirit from me." Why, you may reason, would David even pray such a prayer if the possibility of the Holy Spirit leaving him was not there?

The answer lies in "comparing Scripture with Scripture." In John 14:16–17 Jesus made the following startling statement to His disciples: "And I will pray the Father, and He will give you another Helper, that He may abide with you forever—the Spirit of truth, whom the world cannot receive, because it neither sees Him nor knows Him; but you know Him, for He dwells with you and will be in you." Please notice that in the age (or dispensation) in which the disciples lived—and in which David also lived—the Holy Spirit was with believers, not necessarily in them. However, in the age in which we live, Jesus' promise is that when the Holy Spirit would come on Pentecost (as described in John 7:37–39), He would then dwell within believers, and

His indwelling would be with them forever.

It is important to note that although David was aware he could lose the Holy Spirit, he did not even hint that he might lose his salvation. Because of his prayer, "Restore to me the joy of Your salvation," we see he was fearful of losing "the joy" of God's salvation—not the salvation itself. In the Old Testament, before Christ's promise and before Pentecost, having the Holy Spirit was not the same as having salvation. He could come and go at will and often did.

But in the New Testament, beginning particularly at Pentecost, a believer's relationship with the Holy Spirit changed. At this time Christ said that the Holy Spirit, who used to only dwell with believers temporarily, now dwells in them permanently. In fact, God emphatically says, "Now if anyone does not have the Spirit of Christ, he is not His" (Romans 8:9). After the fulfillment of Christ's promise regarding the coming of the Holy Spirit to indwell believers, there is no suggestion in the New Testament that any believer ever lost the Holy Spirit, or where the Holy Spirit ceased to indwell the believer.

It is sometimes taught that a Christian can grieve away the Holy Spirit. Ephesians 4:30 is often quoted to support this idea. However, there are two important things to observe in this verse: a warning and a promise. First, God's warning is, "And do not grieve the Holy Spirit of God." He does not say, "And do not grieve *away* the Holy Spirit of

God." Scripture supports the idea that the Holy Spirit can be grieved. Does the Scripture teach that a believer today can grieve the Holy Spirit to such a degree that He would leave that one? Absolutely not.

Notice the two parts of this verse: "And do not grieve the Holy Spirit of God by whom you were sealed for the day of redemption." See the warning? Do not grieve the Holy Spirit. See the promise? You are sealed by Him for the day of redemption. God could not guarantee that I am sealed by the Holy Spirit for the day of redemption if it would be possible to grieve away the Spirit before that day. Because of this promise, it is not possible to grieve Him away. However, it is not difficult at all to grieve Him.

The phrase, "Do not grieve the Holy Spirit" is a very intimate one. The greater the love one has for another, the easier it is to be grieved by that one. Any of the things mentioned in Ephesians 4:25–31 grieves the Holy Spirit. God loves us so much that the least little thing in our lives that is out of harmony with His will and character is grievous to Him, so He trains and disciplines us from within. That is how great and faithful our God is.

It is also interesting to note the promise of the Holy Spirit to the believers mentioned in 1 Corinthians. In the first chapter, the book is addressed to all who are saved. In 6:19–20, Paul tells the people that their bodies are the temples of the Holy Spirit. The wording is present tense.

The people to whom he was writing were indwelt by the Holy Spirit—all of them, whether they were obedient to the Lord or disobedient.

What kind of people were they? They were believers (1:2). They had divisions and contentions among them (1:10–11). They were carnal or fleshly, and outwardly their daily walk was no different from unsaved men (3:1–3). Some were puffed up (4:18). At least one of them committed fornication with his stepmother (5:1–5). They were taking one another to court before the unsaved (6:1–7). They were gluttons and getting drunk at the Lord's Table at the time of Communion (11:20–22 and 11:27–30). Others were misusing and abusing spiritual gifts (14:23, 14:32–34, and 14:40), and some did not believe in the literal physical resurrection of Christ from the dead (15:12). Although there were many sins and shortcomings in the Corinthian Christians, they were still Christians indwelt by God the Holy Spirit.

I do not mean to leave the impression that God lightly overlooked their sins. Nothing could be further from the truth. In fact, he told them in 3:16–17 that their bodies were the temples of God, and if they defiled that temple God would destroy them physically. This is an example of the severe chastening of the Lord where he chooses to take one of his children home before his time.

But even though it is a very wicked thing to defile God's temple, Scripture never states that when the Christian sins the Holy Spirit leaves him. Scripture teaches just the opposite—that once we have the Holy Spirit He is in us forever.

I address this issue because the false teaching is so widely spread that salvation and all of its benefits—including having the Holy Spirit—are the result of one's good works. The reality is that the Holy Spirit is given to those who believe. Once He is given to the believer He is in him forever. Therefore, if the believer is ever cast into hell the Holy Spirit would have to be cast into hell with him. What an unthinkable possibility!

How Should I Respond to the Holy Spirit?

If you are a genuine believer in Christ you have the Holy Spirit—all of Him. However, the Holy Spirit does not necessarily have all of you. What I mean by this statement is that although you possess the Holy Spirit, it doesn't necessarily follow that you allow Him to have control over you. Control, you see, is what He desires, but control over our own lives is often the very thing we do not want to relinquish. As a result of the conflict over who controls you, a battle ensues. This battle, which is common to all believers is variously described in the New Testament.

The great apostle Paul described this spiritual struggle several times in his letters. For instance:

For what I am doing, I do not understand. For what I will to do, that I do not practice; but what I hate, that I do. If, then, I do what I will not to do, I agree with the law that it is good. But now, it is no longer I who do it, but sin that dwells in me. For I know that in me (that is, in my flesh) nothing good dwells; for to will is present with me, but how to perform what is good I do not find. For the good that I will to do, I do not do; but the evil I will not to do, that I practice. Now if I do what I will not to do, it is no longer I who do it, but sin that dwells in me. I find then a law, that evil is present with me, the one who wills to do good. For I delight in the law of God according to the inward man. But I see another law in my members, warring against the law of my mind, and bringing me into captivity to the law of sin which is in my members. O wretched man that I am! Who will deliver me from this body of death? I thank God—through Jesus Christ our Lord! So then, with the mind I myself serve the law of God, but with the flesh the law of sin.

Romans 7:15–25

Paul wrote this epistle to the church at Rome some 25 years after his conversion, yet he still faced the same inner struggles and conflicts that we all face. Thank God, though, he discovered his victory was in the Lord, not in himself.

I say then: Walk in the Spirit, and you shall not fulfill the lust of the flesh. For the flesh lusts against the Spirit, and the Spirit against the flesh; and these are contrary to one another, so that you do not do the things that you wish. But if you are led by the Spirit, you are not under the law.

Galatians 5:16–18

If we live in the Spirit, let us also walk in the Spirit.

Galatians 5:25

Here Paul points out that although the Holy Spirit and our flesh nature are constantly at odds with one another (verse 17), our fleshly desires will not gain the upper hand, controlling us, as we walk in (or by means of) the Spirit. And just how do we "walk in the Spirit" rather than after the flesh? Two verses in Romans give clear answers to this important question. In Romans 6:16 it is made clear that to whatever or whomever we yield, we become a slave of that one. "Do you not know that to whom you present yourselves slaves to obey, you are that one's slaves whom you obey, whether of sin leading to death, or of obedience leading to righteousness?" The word "present" in this verse literally means "yield." Therefore, when you yield to the desires of the flesh, you become a slave to those fleshly desires. When you yield to the pressures of the world (see 1 John 2:15–16 for God's description of what constitutes the "world"), you will become worldly in your thinking and actions. When you yield—knowingly or unknowingly—to the deceitful devises of Satan you will become entrapped in his devilish ways. However, when and as you yield to the things of God's Spirit, as revealed in His Word, you will become a voluntary love-slave of His, enjoying spiritual things rather than those things which draw you away from the Lord and His will for you. Be alert, therefore, to whom or what you yield or submit to; it will determine the direction and purpose of your life.

Romans 8:5 adds the thought that whatever occupies our thoughts determines what we become. "For those who live according to the flesh set their minds on the things of the flesh, but those who live according to the Spirit, the things of the Spirit." What makes a weak Christian weak, and a strong Christian strong? Their thought life; those things upon which they dwell in their minds. You can't think all week long about your personal longing for success, or about sex, or dwell upon various personal pleasures— while leaving God out of the picture—and expect to be spiritually minded. It just doesn't happen. Like begets like. You can't be full of worry and anxious thoughts throughout the day and expect to experience God's peace, for the Scripture commands:

> Be anxious for nothing, but in everything by prayer and supplication, with thanksgiving, let your requests be made known to God; and the peace of God, which surpasses all understanding, will guard your hearts and minds through Christ Jesus.
>
> Philippians 4:6–7

This passage makes it clear that as we turn everything over to our Heavenly Father, releasing our own attempts to understand or to control situations or people, His peace becomes a guard or sentry over our "hearts" (the emotional side of us) and our "minds" (our intellects). I've noticed that fears and doubts nearly always creep into our lives either through our emotions or our intellects. For instance, have you ever prayed earnestly for something just "knowing" God would answer the way you wanted Him to, and He didn't? Remember the emotional letdown? Perhaps you even went into a sort of downward spiritual and emotional tailspin. Or perhaps you allowed your disappointment to cause you to doubt God and His goodness. In situations like this we too often feed our doubts and starve our faith, rather than feeding our faith and starving our doubts. Someone wisely observed that "you may not be what you *think* you are, but what you think, you *are*!" Your mind is the real battlefield in the Christian life, so it is imperative to develop the habit of thinking upon spiritual realities and things that are honoring to God.

> Finally, brethren, whatever things are true, whatever things are noble, whatever things are just, whatever things are pure, whatever things are lovely, whatever things are of good report, if there is any virtue and if there is anything praiseworthy—meditate on these things. The things which you learned and received and heard and saw in me, these do, and the God of peace will be with you.
> Philippians 4:8–9

This passage describes exactly the things we are to think upon. Do it and you will be blessed abundantly.

If you are already a believer in Christ, the issue is: "Will you totally yield yourself to the Lord, allowing His Spirit to control your thoughts, desires and life?" If you are willing to submit yourself to Him in this way, it is good to remember that victory in your Christian life depends on your moment-by-moment yieldedness to Him. Otherwise, defeat and discouragement is sure to follow. Failure to surrender yourself to the Lord's leading will not mean you will lose your salvation or the Holy Spirit, but it certainly will result in grieving Him and experiencing a loss of joy and power in your life that you would otherwise be enjoying.

As you "walk in the Spirit" this is the Bible's description of what you can experience in your life: "But the fruit of the Spirit is love, joy, peace, longsuffering, kindness, goodness, faithfulness, gentleness, self-control. Against such there is no law" (Galatians 5:22–23). Pretty desirable and impressive, isn't it? Who wouldn't want such qualities to characterize their life? And it's all yours as you yield to God's Spirit!

Not only may you have "the fruit of the Spirit" in your Christian walk, but you may also enjoy the personal care and nurture of God in your life. This watchfulness over believers is all a part of His ongoing teaching and training of His children—called chastening—which we'll consider next.

God's Chastening

How would you like to know that God is your Heavenly Father and, as such, He faithfully watches over you and cares for your every need? This is exactly how it is with everyone who depends upon Christ for salvation. God promises to train, discipline, or chasten each of His children—out of His infinite love for them.

And you have forgotten the exhortation that speaks to you as to sons; My son, do not despise the chastening of the Lord, nor be discouraged when you are rebuked by Him; for whom the Lord loves He chastens, and scourges every son whom He receives. If you endure chastening, God deals with you as with sons; for what son is there whom a father does not chasten? But if you be without chastening, of which all have become partakers, then you are illegitimate and not sons. Furthermore, we have had human fathers who corrected us, and we paid them respect. Shall we not much more readily be in subjection to the Father of spirits, and live? For they indeed for a few days chastened us as seemed best to them, but He for our profit, that we may be partakers of His holiness. Now no chastening seems to be joyful for the present, but painful; nevertheless afterward it yields the peaceable fruit of righteousness to those who have been trained by it.

Hebrews 12:5–11

Springing out of the new birth is the doctrine of chastening. The word chastening literally means "discipline or training." This 12th chapter of Hebrews is the key passage in the Bible on this subject, and there are some very important things to observe from these verses:

- *The Lord chastens each one of His children because He loves them (verse 6).*

- *If a person does not have chastening from God he is not His child at all, but is illegitimate (verse 8).*

- *God, our Heavenly Father, knows just how to apply chastening to bring about favorable results (verse 10).*

- *Though chastening does not seem good at the time it is administered, it always produces the peaceable fruit of righteousness in those who receive it (verse 11).*

- *Those who know the Lord may "endure chastening" (verse 7); or they may become "discouraged" (faint) under God's chastening hand (verse 5); or they may "despise" the chastening of the Lord (verse 5). In all three cases, however, the people who are chastened are all "sons" (or children of God). If they were not His children they would not be chastened by Him.*

Since it is true that God chastens every child of His, and

the purpose of chastening is to bring about the fruit of righteousness in one's life, we see again that God is the perfect Father.

Remember, one is born into God's family on the sole condition of faith in Jesus Christ. Everyone who is truly born into God's family is also chastened. Because God is the perfect Father, He knows the best way to chasten every one of His children to produce the right kind of life in that son or daughter.

Some say that to teach that one is justified or saved by faith alone is dangerous, because it leads a person to believe in Christ and not care about how he lives—that he will live however he pleases and still go to Heaven. But because God is in charge and trains His children correctly, believers are never left to themselves to just live as they please.

After I received Christ as my Savior I began to be convicted by the Holy Spirit regarding some things in my life—things that I regarded as small and unimportant. When the Lord let me know of things He didn't want me to do, I made one of two choices: either I obeyed the Lord—which brought peace, joy and victory; or I disobeyed Him and was miserable. The Lord—being a faithful and wise Father—would not leave me alone as long as I continued in disobedience. This is what the Bible calls chastening.

Had you asked me soon after I was saved, "Dick, do you live as you please?" I would have replied, "Yes, I do," meaning

I was making my own decisions; I was deciding whether to obey or disobey the Lord; and I was deciding how involved I would be in Christian things. In reality, however, I had many of my attitudes changed by the convicting work of the Holy Spirit and the chastening of my Heavenly Father. All this took place because the new birth is a miraculous reality—not just a theory. My Father had to train, discipline and correct me. He had to keep me in line. If He failed, then He would not have been as good a father as my earthly one.

Is it dangerous to believe that all one has to do is trust in Christ and he can be assured of eternal life? Yes, it is—*if* you only believe in the new birth as a doctrine. But the answer is an emphatic "No" if we take the Biblical viewpoint of the new birth as a miracle from God, and a wonderful reality for the genuine believer.

So if you are already a Christian, choose to endure or yield to the Lord's training in your life and the result will be the "peaceable fruit of righteousness" in your life (verse 11). On the other hand, if you choose not to yield to God's loving, chastening Hand, you will suffer discouragement, defeat and aimlessness because you will have made the choice to "go it alone" without the clear leading and direction that your Heavenly Father longs to provide for you through His Word. It is not a fearful thing to respond in obedience to the Lord's chastening or training. In fact, obeying the Lord as He attempts to train you is the safest and best thing for you personally. Think about it: if God loves you (and He does) and knows your future, and longs to provide the best and happiest future for you, if only you will allow Him to; where is the downside? There is none. Will it always be easy? Of course not, but life is not easy. However, as you allow Him to guide and teach you, you will benefit a hundred times over and will begin to absolutely love your relationship with the Lord.

Somehow Christians have gotten the impression that to totally surrender their lives to God is a very dreadful, unpleasant thing to do. We reason, "If I give my entire life over to the Lord, He's going to lead me to the most primitive, backward and dangerous place on earth, with no electricity or indoor bathrooms! And it will probably be 100+ degrees in the shade all year long, with huge spiders and deadly snakes everywhere; and I'll have to eat the most repulsive wormy food imaginable." Such a concept is far from what the Bible teaches concerning God's methods and motives in chastening or training His children.

First, I remind you, it is "whom the Lord loves He chastens," not whom He hates. An infinitely loving God would never do anything unloving to His child. That's not to say that He would never lead you to do difficult or unpleasant things. Even on the human level, good parents will sometimes have their children do things outside of their comfort zones in order to stretch them and mature them.

God often does the same thing, only better than any human parent could do (read Hebrews 11:9–10).

Secondly, consider this fact: Psalm 37:4 promises, "Delight yourself also in the LORD, and He shall give you the desires of your heart." Does such a promise sound "dreadful" or "unpleasant?" Actually, it sounds pretty great, doesn't it? But let's not jump to any wrong conclusions. Notice there is a condition to be met to have "the desires of your heart" given to you. And what is that condition? "Delight yourself in the LORD." What exactly does that mean? Well, if you delight yourself in another person, what does that entail? Wouldn't it include pleasing that one, caring for him or her—enough to put their wishes and needs before your own? If you don't think so, you have never truly "delighted" yourself in anyone other than yourself.

When you do delight in another, your previous desires, and even your reasons for living, may begin changing you into a different person with different aspirations and goals. The same is true when you delight in the God who saved you. In fact, some have pointed out that the phrase, "He shall give you the desires of your heart" might also read, "He shall give you the desires for your heart." That is, as you delight in Him, He changes your desires to conform to His desires for you. You may find it difficult to grasp, but there are even believers who have come to love "the most primitive, backward and dangerous places on earth." They delighted in their Lord and He instilled in them a love and longing for people in such circumstances—people who have never been exposed to the Gospel of God's amazing grace.

The important thing to remember, however, is that delighting in the Lord is the best and safest way to go. The desires that will then be realized will be the most noble and satisfying to you, and as God gives them to you He will be glorified. That's chastening working in you as it should— God doing the training and you doing the delighting, responding and learning as He graciously leads you along through life.

As you allow Him the freedom to mold you, you will enjoy a healthy time of spiritual growth, which is our topic in Chapter Five.

Growing in Grace

It is normal for a newborn baby to grow. Failure to do so indicates some very severe problems. In the same way, those who become children of God through faith in Christ are expected, encouraged, and empowered to grow in their spiritual lives. Growth in the Christian life, as in the physical life, is usual and desirable. A growing relationship of any kind is one in which there will be a sense of closeness and a deepening love and respect. So it is in the believer's walk with the Lord. Such growth is not automatic in the Christian's life, but it is expected; it is normal. As mentioned previously, as God's child responds to His training, fruits of righteousness will be produced.

> But grow in the grace and knowledge of our Lord and Savior Jesus Christ. To Him be the glory both now and forever. Amen.
>
> 2 Peter 3:18

> For we are his workmanship, created in Christ Jesus for good works, which God prepared beforehand that we should walk in them.
>
> Ephesians 2:10

> This is a faithful saying, and these things I want you to affirm

constantly, that those who have believed in God should be careful to maintain good works. These things are good and profitable to men.

Titus 3:8

It is God's grace by which we are saved, and it is God's grace that teaches us to live godly lives.

For the grace of God that brings salvation has appeared to all men, teaching us that, denying ungodliness and worldly lusts, we should live soberly, righteously, and godly, in the present age.

Titus 2:11–12

By His grace He enables us through the Holy Spirit to live differently than before we knew Him.

For sin shall not have dominion over you, for you are not under law but under grace.

Romans 6:14

Growing into a mature Christian is rewarding, both now in this life and when we are with the Lord in the future. In the first chapter of 2 Peter we are given some great promises and guidance. In verse three it's revealed that we have "His divine power" by which has been "given to us all things that pertain to life and godliness." Verse four reminds us of "exceedingly great and precious promises" through which we have been made "partakers of the divine nature." So, as a believer in Christ you have God's divine power and His divine nature in you to enable you to walk in a godly way.

Beginning in verse five, we are told to "add" to our faith certain virtues or characteristics. The fact that we who are already God's children are admonished to add these qualities to our faith clearly demonstrates that such virtues are not automatically produced in a believer's life. We are to add them, and then we are reminded what the results will be.

The characteristics are listed in verses 5–7, where we are urged to diligently add them to add to our faith:

Virtue (verse 5)
A quality or disposition in which goodness characterizes one's life; speaks of high moral standards, integrity, honor and respectability.

Knowledge (verse 5)
This is knowledge of the Lord (3:18), which is the result of diligent study of His Word and a personal application of it to life.

Self-control (verse 6)
First-hand knowledge of Scripture leads us on to progressive growth in controlling emotions, thoughts, and actions.

Perseverance (verse 6)
Patience, growing out of self-control and producing the

capacity to endure difficulties and afflictions.

Godliness (verse 6)
Inner Christlikeness; a believer who is abiding in Christ
and, thus, is at rest in the Lord no matter what the
circumstances.

Brotherly kindness (verse 7)
Love for fellow believers because they are fellow members of
the same divine Family.

Love (verse 7)
Love for everyone, including the world outside the bonds of
the Christian family.

One virtue seems to flow into another, and that one into
another, and so spiritual growth deepens more and more
along our spiritual journey.

Now notice the results if we add these qualities to our
faith.

> For if these things are yours and abound, you will be neither barren
> nor unfruitful in the knowledge of our Lord Jesus Christ. For he
> who lacks these things is shortsighted, even to blindness, and has
> forgotten that he was cleansed from his old sins. Therefore, brethren,
> be even more diligent to make your call and election sure, for if you
> do these things you will never stumble; for so an entrance will be

supplied to you abundantly into the everlasting kingdom of our Lord and Savior Jesus Christ.

2 Peter 1:8–11

What of those believers who do not add "these things" to their faith? By implication, verse eight assumes they will be barren and unproductive, and verse ten indicates the real possibility that such immature believers will stumble and fall. The same verse also suggests that since an abundant entrance is promised to the believer who adds "these things" to his faith, it seems obvious that the believer who refuses to grow in his faith will not have an abundant entrance into God's everlasting kingdom. Verse nine adds the sad (but true) judgment that "he who lacks these things is shortsighted, even to blindness, and has forgotten that he was purged [cleansed] from his old sins."

If we stop growing in our Christian walk, we go backwards and the sense of closeness with the Lord will vanish; that is, until we begin again to allow His grace to teach us through His Word and to respond as we should in obedience. That's when growth will be reestablished and our walk with Him will be the normal and satisfying relationship that He longs for us to enjoy.

When you trust in the unmerited favor of God, a strange and miraculous thing happens. He provides for growth in your life and as you yield to Him, you will begin to experience—by His grace—victory over sin. Having victory through grace is the way the Christian life was intended to be lived.

The Spirit of grace is what enables us to grow. It is through His grace that we progress in our Christian lives as we should, not through the letter of the Law. John 1:17 declares: "For the law was given through Moses, but grace and truth came through Jesus Christ." In light of the fact that "grace and truth" came through Christ, take this passage to heart: "Not that we are sufficient of ourselves to think of anything as being from ourselves, but our sufficiency is from God who also made us sufficient as ministers of the new covenant, not of the letter but of the Spirit; for the letter kills, but the Spirit gives life" (2 Corinthians 3:5–6).

Some say that God's grace is His love in action. The following passage seems to convey this thought:

> For the love of Christ compels us, because we judge thus: that if One died for all, then all died; and He died for all, that those who live should live no longer for themselves, but for Him who died for them and rose again.
>
> 2 Corinthians 5:14–15

Notice that it is because we already have life that we should live for Him. It does not say we should live for Him to gain eternal life. That would be putting the cart before the horse.

What a difference between living legally under the Law and living freely under grace!

The apostle Paul asked the Galatian believers, "Are you so foolish? Having begun in the Spirit, are you now being made perfect by the flesh?" The anticipated answer is, "Of course not!" Later Paul added:

> Stand fast therefore in the liberty by which Christ has made us free, and do not be entangled again with a yoke of bondage [the Mosaic Law].
>
> Galatians 5:1

> For you, brethren, have been called to liberty; only do not use liberty as an opportunity for the flesh, but through love serve one another.
>
> Galatians 5:13

Grace is often the opposite of law. The Mosaic Law said, "Do, and you shall live." Grace, on the other hand, declares, "Because you are already spiritually alive, obey Me." Unfortunately many Christians, often without realizing it, live as if they are under law. They think, "I was saved by grace, but I mature or grow in my walk with the Lord by performing." It is true that obedience pleases the Lord, but your motive in obeying Him determines whether you live a joyful, victorious life, or suffer defeat after defeat. Colossians 2:6 reminds us of the importance, even the necessity, of living for Christ in the same manner as we initially came to Him. It says: "As you have therefore received Christ Jesus the Lord, so walk in Him." How did you receive Him? Ephesians 2:8 reminds us we received him "by grace through faith." According to Colossians 2:6 how should you now walk "in Him"? The same way you received Him—by grace through faith. Walking by faith while trusting in the grace of God to enable you is the Christian life in a nutshell.

These great truths should compel us—out of gratitude for already having salvation—to want to please Him who died for us. Thankfulness to God for such a great salvation is the heartbeat of Christian growth.

Not only does God graciously guide His teachable children, He even rewards them for following Him. Let's talk about that some.

Rewards

Overall, it seems little is being taught about rewards in Christian circles, and when the subject is considered it is sometimes not dealt with from a truly Biblical perspective. It is important—and it will prove so beneficial—to approach the topic of rewards from a Biblical viewpoint. In doing so I will share a few essential Scriptural insights that have helped me through the years to gain a firm grasp of this key truth.

Rewards Are Earned

It is important to realize that, unlike salvation which is a gift, rewards are earned; they are not freely given to all. God's Word states, "Do not be deceived, God is not mocked; for whatever a man sows, that he will also reap" (Galatians 6:7). You earn a crop; it is not just handed to you. In verses nine and ten the apostle Paul wrote, "And let us not grow weary while doing good, for in due season we shall reap if we do not lose heart. Therefore, as we have opportunity, let us do good to all, especially to those who are of the household of faith." There must be the sowing before there is the reaping, but the reaping certainly does come. It is determined by what is sown and how the seed is cared for or managed. The crop is the reward for one's diligence and effort.

A good example of rewards being earned rather than being outright gifts is the parable of the minas recorded in Luke 19:11–27. In this parable Jesus mentioned a nobleman going on a long journey and giving one mina to each of ten servants (verses 12–13). Each mina was worth about three month's salary. Upon returning from his journey, he called the servants together "that he might know how much every man had gained by trading." One servant had gained ten minas for one; another gained five minas for one (verses 15–19). The nobleman rewarded both of these faithful servants by giving them authority over ten and five cities respectively (verses 16–19). But there was a third servant who did nothing. He simply held on to the one mina his master had originally given him. To this servant the nobleman responded with this stinging rebuke: "Out of your own mouth I will judge you, you wicked servant" (verse 22). He then commanded that because this servant had not multiplied the one mina, it should be taken from him and given to the one who had ten (verses 23–24). The lesson of the parable is given in verse 26: "I say to you, that to everyone who has will be given; and from him who does not have, even what he has will be taken away from him."

The reward of ruling over cities was obviously earned by the faithful and wise investment the two servants made, while what could have been a reward to the third servant was denied and given to another.

Concerning sowing and reaping you can put it down as an ironclad rule that you reap *what* you sow; you reap *more* than you sow; and you reap *later* than you sow.

Rewards Are Only for Believers in Christ

They are not offered to anyone else. God does not promise any rewards for unbelievers. Paul was speaking to fellow believers in Romans 14:10–12 when he said:

> But why do you judge your brother? Or why do you show contempt for your brother? For we shall all stand before the judgment seat of Christ. For it is written: "As I live, says the Lord, every knee shall bow to Me, and every tongue shall confess to God." So then each of us shall give account of himself to God.

He further elaborates on this theme in 1 Corinthians 3:11–15. He emphasizes in verse 11 that there is only one foundation upon which believers may build—the Lord Jesus Christ. On this foundation each believer may build works that are described as either "gold, silver or precious stones" or "wood, hay or straw." Those who build things of high quality (the gold, silver and precious stones) will receive a reward (verse 14). But such a reward is reserved for believers in Christ and no one else.

Rewards Are Based Upon the Believer's Works After Salvation

Notice the emphasis upon the believer's works in the following passages.

> Each one's work will become clear; for the Day will declare it, because it will be revealed by fire; and the fire will test each one's work, of what sort it is. If anyone's work which he has built on it endures, he will receive a reward. If anyone's work is burned he will suffer loss; but he himself will be saved, yet so as through fire.
>
> 1 Corinthians 3:13–15

> For we must all appear before the judgment seat of Christ, that each one may receive the things done in the body, according to what he has done, whether good or bad.
>
> 2 Corinthians 5:10

Rewards Are Based Upon the Quality of a Believer's Works

Every believer will stand before the Judgment Seat of Christ. This is an evaluation judgment, revealing the quality of our works, whether little or much. The last phrase of 1 Corinthians 3:13 makes this clear when it says, "and the fire will test each one's work, of what sort it is." *Sort* speaks of quality, not necessarily of quantity. God is more interested in the value of our works than in the quantity of them, though this does not mean that small equals quality and large equals inferior works. There may be value or no value in much or little. Therefore the character of the work is what determines its worth.

Rewards Are Based on the Christian's Words, Thoughts, and Hidden Motives

Not only will the Christian's works be exposed and evaluated, but also his words, thoughts and hidden motives will be judged. This may be the scariest part of having our lives weighed before Christ.

Jesus Himself stated, "I say to you that for every idle word men may speak, they will give an account of it in the day of judgment" (Matthew 12:36).

At another time He said, "There is nothing hidden which will not be revealed, nor has anything been kept secret but that it should come to light" (Mark 4:22).

The apostle Paul adds this: "Therefore judge nothing before the time, until the Lord comes, who will both bring to light the hidden things of darkness and reveal the counsels [motives] of the hearts" (1 Corinthians 4:5).

Add to all of the above this very solemn revelation in

Hebrews 4:13 concerning how God sees us: "There is no creature hidden from His sight, but all things are naked and open to the eyes of Him to whom we must give account."

Rewards Will Not Be Given to All Believers

Some will lose rewards they could have had, while others may lose rewards they may already have had at one time. All such Christians will feel shame before their Lord when He comes for them. Referring back to 1 Corinthians 3 again, verse 15 states, "If anyone's work is burned, he will suffer loss; but he himself will be saved, yet so as through fire." In context the word "loss" has to do with loss of rewards, and the word "burned" in the verse means to be completely burned down with nothing left. So the loss would be complete loss of any reward if what one builds upon the foundation of Christ is nothing but wood, hay and straw. It will be a pretty drastic time for some. Two of the letters of the apostle John also reveals some sobering thoughts upon this topic. In 2 John 8 he writes, "Look to yourselves that we do not lose those things we worked for, but that we may receive a full reward." Earlier, in 1 John 2:28, he says this to his spiritual children, "And now, little children, abide in Him, that when He appears, we may have confidence and not be ashamed before Him at His coming." God adds a further warning in Revelation 3:11 in a letter to the church in Philadelphia, where He says, "Behold, I come quickly! Hold fast what you have, that no one may take your crown [speaking of reward]."

An Inheritance in Christ's Earthly Kingdom Will Not Be Given to All Believers

Although all believers in Christ enter God's spiritual kingdom the moment they believe in Him, and though all believers will enter the physical earthly kingdom of God in the future, not all will have an inheritance in His earthly kingdom. In other words, only faithful believers will have an inheritance in the kingdom of God, ruling and reigning with Christ during His 1,000 year reign on earth. Many believers have never even considered this possibility that we all may be in the kingdom, but not all will be enjoying rewards there; that is, having an inheritance. Consider the following verses.

In Matthew 25:14–28 (similar to the parable of the minas in Luke) Jesus begins the parable by saying, "The kingdom of heaven is like a man traveling to a far country, who called his own servants and delivered his goods to them." To one he gave five talents (money), to another two and to another one. The servants who had five and two talents each doubled the amount they had when their lord returned from his journey. To each of these he said, "Well done, good and faithful servant; you were faithful over a few things, I will make you ruler over many things. Enter into the joy of your lord" (verses 21–23). The remaining servant did nothing with his lord's money and suffered severely for it, losing even the one talent he had been given and ending up being labeled as an "unprofitable servant" who will weep and gnash his teeth (verses 24–30).

Romans 8:16–17 contains one of the most neglected truths along this line. People seem to just fly by it as they read it without the solemnity of the statement sinking in. The apostle wrote: "The Spirit Himself bears witness with our spirit that we are children of God, and if children, then heirs—heirs of God and joint heirs with Christ, if indeed we suffer with Him, that we may also be glorified together." Do you see the possible distinction between being an heir of God and a joint heir with Christ? If we are God's child then we are an heir of His; we are a joint heir with Christ if we suffer with Him. Not all Christians suffer with Christ even though we are appointed to it.[9] On the contrary, I'm afraid many of God's children do all they can to avoid any kind of suffering or persecution that is related to their faith in Christ.

Revelation 20:4 describes those who will be beheaded "for their witness to Jesus and for the word of God, who had not worshipped the beast or his image, and had not received his mark on their foreheads or on their hands. And they lived and reigned with Christ for a thousand years." Who does it say will live and reign with Christ for a thousand years? Those who were faithful to their martyred deaths. This certainly does not describe all believers, does it? Some of God's children will reign in the kingdom while others will be there but not be reigning.

There Are Different Rewards Given for Various Kinds of Faithful Service

The Imperishable Crown
"And everyone who competes for the prize is temperate [self-controlled] in all things. Now they do it to obtain a perishable crown, but we for an imperishable crown" (1 Corinthians 9:25).

This crown is for those Christians who live self-controlled, disciplined lives. A good example of a disciplined attitude was expressed to me years ago this way: "Pray when you feel like it, pray when you don't feel like it, and pray until you do feel like it!" Another Biblical way to view it is in Christ's question to His disciples in Luke 6:46 when He said, "Why do you call Me 'Lord, Lord,' and do not do the things which I say?"

The Crown of Rejoicing
"What is our hope, or joy, or crown of rejoicing? Is it not even

you in the presence of our Lord Jesus Christ at His coming? For you are our glory and joy" (1 Thessalonians 2:19–20).

Paul considered those whom he had won to Christ to be his crown at the coming of the Lord, so some have called this the Soul Winner's Crown.

The Crown of Righteousness

"I have fought the good fight, I have finished the race, I have kept the faith. Finally, there is laid up for me the crown of righteousness, which the Lord, the righteous Judge, will give to me on that Day, and not to me only but also to all who have loved His appearing" (2 Timothy 4:7–8).

It appears that the evidence or proof that one "loves His appearing" is that the qualities Paul mentions in verse seven are characteristic of the believer—"fighting the good fight," by which I think he is referring to what Jude calls "contending for the faith" (Jude 3); "finishing the race" which indicates steadfastness in fulfilling God's purpose throughout one's entire Christian life; and "keeping the faith" which may be another way of expressing our loyalty to God's truth without compromise. Such a committed child of God will naturally be longing for the Lord's return, loving His appearance. Others, less dedicated, will not be too eager to meet the Lord face to face.

The Crown of Life

"Blessed is the man who endures temptation [or trials]; for when he has been approved, he will receive the crown of life which the Lord has promised to those who love Him" (James 1:12).

As with the crown of righteousness, it seems that the genuine evidence of truly loving the Lord Jesus Christ is the believer's willingness to go through trials, even severe ones, for His sake. How much I am willing to suffer for Him is the measure of my love for Him.

The Crown of Glory

"Shepherd the flock of God which is among you, serving as overseers, not by compulsion but willingly, not for dishonest gain but eagerly; nor as being lords over those entrusted to you, but being examples to the flock; and when the Chief Shepherd appears, you will receive the crown of glory that does not fade away" (1 Peter 5:2-4).

This crown is for faithful shepherds over the flock of God. In verses 1–3, Peter, a fellow elder, admonished other elders to be good shepherds over the local flocks which God had put under their charge. He tells them not to serve "by compulsion but willingly;" and "not for dishonest gain but eagerly." They were not to be "lords over" those entrusted to them, but to be "examples to the flock." Then he gave this promise: "and when the Chief Shepherd appears, you will receive the crown of glory that does not fade away." If God has placed you over a group of fellow believers—entrusting to you their spiritual care—then you may qualify for this crown of glory by being the kind of under-shepherd that God describes in this passage. Though addressed to "elders" or pastors, I think it is safe to apply the principles here to anyone to whom God has entrusted the spiritual care of some of His sheep.

Different crowns or rewards for various areas of loyalty to the Lord will be given to those who qualify. May we all seek to be crowned because such crowns "in the sweet by and by" will be evidences of the love and loyalty to the Lord we had "in the nasty here and now." Crowns for us will bring glory to Him as indicated in Revelation 4:10–11:

> The twenty-four elders fall down before Him who sits on the throne and worship Him who lives forever and ever, and cast their crowns before the throne, saying: 'You are worthy, O Lord, to receive glory and honor and power; for You created all things, and by Your will they exist and were created.

Rewards Are Based Upon Each Believer's Capacity, Knowledge, or Ability

The rewards are fairly distributed based upon what God has imparted to each of His children and their response to

His provision. Luke 12:35–48 is a very revealing passage that teaches this truth. In giving this parable, Jesus emphasized faithful and unfaithful servants who either serve Him or who do not. I want us to pick up the story in verses 45–47:

> But if that servant says in his heart, "My master is delaying his coming," and begins to beat the male and female servants, and to eat and drink and be drunk, the master of that servant will come on a day when he is not looking for him, and at an hour when he is not aware, and will cut him in two and appoint him his portion with the unbelievers [literally, the unfaithful]. And that servant who knew his master's will, and did not prepare himself or do according to his will, shall be beaten with many stripes.

So far in the parable we have an illustration of one who was well aware of what his master expected of him, but did just the opposite of that. The result was that he suffered severely for his laxness and unfaithfulness. But what of a servant who may not know what his master expects? Will he be dealt with in the same way? Jesus goes on to say this in verse 48:

> But he who did not know, yet committed things deserving of stripes, shall be beaten with few. For everyone to whom much is given, from him much will be required; and to whom much has been committed, of him they will ask the more.

That last sentence is the point of the entire parable. The more knowledge we have of God's will, the more accountable we are to obey it. God is completely just in the manner in which He metes out or withholds blessings and rewards.

This same principle is also mentioned in James 3:1 where it says, "My brethren, let not many of you become teachers, knowing that we shall receive a stricter judgment." The more we know, the more accountable we are to live up to that knowledge. This being true, it is foolish to compare ourselves or our ministries to others. In fact, God warns of doing so in 2 Corinthians 10:12:

> For we dare not class ourselves or compare ourselves with those who commend themselves. But they, measuring themselves by themselves, and comparing themselves among themselves, are not wise.

We are each responsible to live up to the light that we have, and to use what gifts or abilities God has given us. That's all. What God does with others, or how He chooses to use them, is really none of our concern. We should focus on whether or not we are doing His will as we understand that will.

Serving the Lord for Rewards Is a Proper and Legitimate Motivation

There are at least two reasons why this is so. First, we've already seen that Jesus Himself used the reward motive over and over again when He taught on the necessity of faithfulness on the part of His children. Consider any of the parable passages we've already covered to see this. Secondly, God gives us the example of none other than the great lawgiver, Moses, to illustrate the legitimacy of serving Him for the prospect of future rewards. Here's what Hebrews 11:24–26 records:

> By faith Moses, when he became of age, refused to be called the son of Pharaoh's daughter, choosing rather to suffer affliction with the people of God than to enjoy the passing pleasures of sin, esteeming the reproach of Christ greater riches than the treasures in Egypt; for he looked to the reward.

Years ago I knew a man who scorned the idea of serving Christ for reward. He felt it was a carnal and unspiritual reason for serving the Lord, yet the chorus of his favorite hymn said, "It will be worth it all when we see Jesus!" Doesn't that express the thought of being somehow rewarded when we see Him?

I think the apostle Paul expressed this sentiment quite well in two of his letters. In Romans 8:18 he wrote, "For I consider that the sufferings of this present time are not worthy to be compared with the glory which shall be revealed in us." And what was it that Moses was willing to endure for future reward? Doesn't Hebrews say he chose to "suffer affliction with the people of God than to enjoy the passing pleasures of sin, esteeming the reproach of Christ greater riches than the treasures in Egypt?"

Later, Paul wrote:

> For our light affliction, which is but for a moment, is working for us a far more exceeding and eternal weight of glory, while we do not look at the things which are seen, but at the things which are not seen. For the things which are seen are temporary, but the things which are not seen are eternal.
>
> 2 Corinthians 4:17–18

Rewards Are a Phenomenal Demonstration of God's Amazing Grace

God evidences His grace to us by:

- *Clearly revealing His will in His Word, so we are not in the dark as to what He expects from us.*[10]

- *Equipping or gifting each one of us so that we may serve Him effectively.*[11]

- *Empowering each believer by His Holy Spirit to enable us to obey His will.*[12]

So here's the picture: God tells us what to do, fully equips us to do it, empowers us from within so that we need not fail, and then—on top of all that—He rewards us for doing it! If that isn't grace, I don't know what is!

No Excuses

In light of all we know about rewards, there is no excuse for any child of God to hold back from totally devoting himself or herself to the Lord. I realize that we give many seemingly plausible excuses for our failure to be fully surrendered to Christ, but that's all they are—excuses. I will examine some of them and give a scriptural response to each.

Temptations Are So Great

"No temptation has overtaken you except as is common to man; but God is faithful, who will not allow you to be tempted beyond what you are able, but with the temptation will also make the way of escape, that you may be able to bear it" (1 Corinthians 10:13).

Sin Is Everywhere

"For as by one man's [Adam's] disobedience many were made sinners, so also by one Man's [Christ's] obedience many will be made righteous. Moreover the law entered that the offense might abound. But where sin abounded, grace abounded much more, so that as sin reigned in death, even so grace might reign through righteousness to eternal life through Jesus Christ our Lord" (Romans 5:19–21).

"Therefore do not let sin reign in your mortal body, that you should obey it in its lusts. And do not present your members as instruments of unrighteousness to sin, but present yourselves to God as being alive from the dead, and your members as instruments of righteousness to God.For sin shall not have dominion over you, for you are not under the law but under grace" (Romans 6:12-14).

I Am So Weak in My Flesh

"I say then: Walk in the Spirit and you shall not fulfill the lust of the flesh" (Galatians 5:16).

"Watch and pray, lest you enter into temptation. The spirit indeed is willing, but the flesh is weak" (Matthew 26:41).

Even High-Profile Christian Leaders Fail, So How Can There Be Hope For Me?

"Fear not, for I am with you; be not dismayed, for I am your God. I will strengthen you, yes, I will help you, I will uphold you with My righteous right hand" (Isaiah 41:10).

It Is So Hard to Live the Christian Life

"Come to Me, all you who labor and are heavy laden, and I will give you rest. Take My yoke upon you and learn from Me, for I am gentle and lowly in heart, and you will find rest for your souls. For My yoke is easy and My burden is light" (Matthew 11:28–30).

Rather than making excuses for not serving the Lord, rejoice in that He is totally adequate to save us, keep us, discipline us, and use us. Then, if we allow Him to use us, He will reward us, both now and in eternity. The key is our own submission to Him. This verse says it about as clearly as any I know: "Do you not know that to whom you present [yield] yourselves slaves to obey, you are that one's slaves whom you obey, whether of sin leading to death, or of obedience leading to righteousness" (Romans 6:16). Whatever or to whomever you yield yourself, you become that one's slave. Therefore, dear child of God, habitually yield or submit yourself to the Lord. As you do, great blessing will be yours now and certain future rewards will follow.

The Security of the Believer

There is sometimes great confusion and uneasiness among many professed Christians as to how certain a believer may be of his or her salvation. But make no mistake about it, once a person has trusted Christ he or she is completely secure in Christ. Once a person is a child of God nothing can ever change that. Many people have doubts about their salvation, some do not know the Bible teaches you are secure forever, and some deny that you are secure.

Can the Believer Be Confident of His Salvation?

> And I give them eternal life, and they shall never perish; neither shall anyone snatch them out of My hand. My Father, who has given them to Me, is greater than all; and no one is able to snatch them out of My Father's hand.
>
> John 10:28–29

> All that the Father gives Me will come to Me, and the one who comes to Me I will by no means cast out. For I have come down from heaven, not to do My own will, but the will of Him who sent Me.

> This is the will of the Father who sent Me, that of all He has given Me I should lose nothing, but should raise it up at the last day.
>
> John 6:37–39

> These things I have written to you who believe in the name of the Son of God, that you may know that you have eternal life.
>
> 1 John 5:13

Notice closely the words: *never*, *lose nothing*, and *know*. God's promise is clear—a believer shall never perish; God will not lose him; he can know he has eternal life. We are able to have complete confidence and assurance of our salvation because it is dependent on God's provision in Christ. God says in 1 John 2:2 and 4:10 that Christ's death was the satisfaction for my sin. Because God is satisfied with Christ's sin payment, then after I have trusted in Christ I need not ever doubt that I am His. But many people do doubt because of misconceptions, false teaching or ignorance. We'll now look at some of the more common misunderstandings concerning the security of the believer.

Can a Christian Who is Unproductive Still be Saved?

First Corinthians 3:11–16 speaks of the believer's works. It begins by discussing the foundation that has been laid in a believer's life. Jesus Christ alone is the foundation of my salvation—never something earned or a reward for something done. Verse 11 says, "For no other foundation can anyone lay than that which is laid, which is Jesus Christ." The foundation for salvation is Jesus Christ—only Christ.

Once you put your faith in Him you are placed upon the foundation and may then build upon Christ. The idea of building upon Christ does not imply that there is something about Him or His work that needs improvement. Christ is the foundation. When you build upon that foundation you are not improving the foundation; you are building something upon a Perfect Foundation. You may build something good and profitable or something worthless upon this foundation (verse 12). But that "building" does not put you on the foundation nor does it keep you there. Once you are on the foundation you are on it to stay, even though what you may build will not have much value.

Verse 12 says that those who know the Lord may build upon the foundation of Christ "gold, silver, precious stones, wood, hay [or] straw." In verse 13, God tells us that the work of everyone who is on the foundation will "become clear" or be revealed. It will be revealed by fire to demonstrate the quality of it—how much value it has. The last part of verse 13 says, "The fire will test each one's work, of what sort it is." "Sort" speaks of the quality of the work rather than the quantity; the kind of work a Christian produces rather than the amount.

Those believers who build from materials that withstand the fire ("gold, silver, and precious stones") will receive a reward. Fire purifies these stones (verse 14). However, the Christian who lives carelessly will have his work "burned"—completely burned down (described as "wood, hay and straw"). When fire is applied to these types of materials they burn up. Thus, we see that the Christian whose life is unfruitful shall have his unfruitful work burned. The result will be that he will suffer loss.

> If anyone's work is burned, he will suffer loss; but he himself will be saved, yet so as through fire. Do you not know that you are the temple of God and that the Spirit of God dwells in you?
>
> 1 Corinthians 3:15–16

What about his salvation? Surely God could not allow a Christian to constantly be unproductive in his life and still be saved. God Himself gives the answer: "He will suffer loss: but he himself will be saved, yet so as through fire" (verse 15). Notice carefully the three things that are true of the Christian whose works are "wood, hay and straw":

1. *His work will be burned.*

2. *He will suffer loss.*

3. *The man himself will be saved.*

A man who builds bad works on the foundation of Christ will still be saved but will suffer loss. However, "suffering loss" is not the only thing that happens when a Christian fails to build in fruitful ways. There are also other sad results of not living for the Lord: unnecessary discipline from God, the loss of joy, reaping the results of what you sow, and purposelessness with its accompanying misery. Also, there will be that dreaded time when such a Christian must stand before the Lord face to face to "receive the things done in the body, whether good or bad" (2 Corinthians 5:10). As I have already mentioned, Scripture points out in 1 John 2:28 that there will be some of God's children who, instead of being confident at the coming of the Lord, will stand before Him "ashamed."

God deals with the lack of faithfulness in His children in many ways. One way will be a future loss. Just what that "loss" will entail we may not be able to say for certain, but we can say that it will not involve a loss of salvation. Never forget it—"He will suffer loss: but he himself will be saved." However, the loss that he will suffer apparently will be most unpleasant, because God says that the unfaithful Christian will be saved, "yet so as through fire." When describing such a man today, we would probably use the phrase that he would be saved "by the skin of his teeth."

All of us who know the Lord should desire to be as fruitful as possible. Since Jesus Christ is God, and He gave

Himself for me, I could never do enough for Him. The motive behind my service, however, should be that of gratitude and love to the Lord—never any idea of earning or meriting His favor. However, we do have the added blessing of His promise to us of rewards for any good and faithful service to Him. As believers, we should have the perspective expressed in the following:

> *Only one life 'twill soon be past;*
> *Only what's done for Christ will last.*

Now let's look at John 15:1–6. If God chastens or trains every child He receives as we discussed in Chapter Four, what about that one who despises His chastening—the one who shows no outward evidence of yielding to the Lord's training?

First of all, we must realize that we cannot afford to deal in what "appears to be." A person may "appear" not to be producing fruit, or they may "appear" to not be undergoing any chastening of the Lord, but in both cases our powers of observation may be wrong or limited. We do not know what's going on inside of another person—in his heart—but God does.

As mentioned earlier, we are not saved or kept saved by good works, but the normal Christian life should produce good works. (Read again Hebrews 12:11; Ephesians 2:10; and

Titus 3:8). However, the Scriptures do record that there can be extreme cases where a genuine believer does not produce good works. The result of such a fruitless life is to be taken home prematurely—not a pleasant thought at all.

John 15:1–5 describes four kinds of Christians (called "branches" in this chapter):

> I [Christ] am the true vine, and My Father is the vinedresser. Every branch in me that does not bear fruit He takes away: and every branch that bears fruit He prunes, that it may bear more fruit. You are already clean because of the word which I have spoken to you. Abide in Me, and I in you. As the branch cannot bear fruit of itself, unless it abides in the vine, neither can you, unless you abide in Me. I am the vine, you are the branches. He who abides in me, and I in him, bears much fruit; for without Me you can do nothing.

Notice the four kinds of branches, or believers: There are those who bear no fruit (verse 2), those who bear fruit (verse 2), those who bear more fruit (verse 2), and those who bear much fruit (verse 5). The standard (not the average) for the Christian should be much fruit (called elsewhere "hundredfold" fruit). The majority of Christians probably fall in the middle two categories—those who bear fruit and those who bear more fruit. The extreme case is the believer who does not bear any fruit. Most Christians would say that such a person is not even saved, but Jesus Christ referred to them as "every branch in Me that does not bear fruit." So this person is saved because he is "in Christ."

The result of a person who bears no fruit at all is that the Father takes him away (verse 2). The words "takes away" literally mean "takes up." So, what does the Father do with any children who refuse to bear fruit, and who despise His chastening? He takes them up; that is, he takes them home before their time. Ecclesiastes 7:17 says "Do not be overly wicked, nor be foolish: Why should you die before your time?"

An example of this is 1 Corinthians 11 where God describes Christians who partook of the Lord's Supper unworthily. He says regarding these disobedient believers, "For this reason many are weak and sick among you, and many sleep [are dead]" (1 Corinthians 11:30). It is a punishment—not a reward—to have to face God prematurely. I would hate to stand before the Lord and answer Him face to face as to why I did not produce fruit for Him, and why I despised His chastening.

If you are already a child of God through faith in Christ, choose to accept the Lord's training in your life. Respond to it by learning the lessons He has for you that will make you more like Christ.

If I Sin Will I Lose My Salvation?

Some say one may lose his salvation if he sins too much and is not growing in his Christian life. The question is, how much can one sin and still be saved? Where do you draw the line between sinning and being allowed by God to stay in His family, or of sinning too much and therefore being cast out of His family? Of course, such a thing cannot happen, for Christ's promise is sure. He said, "He who believes in Me has everlasting life" (John 6:47).

Before a person is saved, bad works do not send him to hell and good works do not save him. After a person is saved, bad works do not send him to hell and good works do not keep him saved. Works—good or bad—have nothing to do either with obtaining salvation or retaining it. My spiritual growth does not determine if I keep my salvation.

I received Christ as my Savior in 1953. I may not now be all that I should be for the Lord, but I have grown some in the last 50-plus years in my walk with Christ. Those who believe that a saved man can lose his salvation, for all practical purposes, do not leave any room in the Christian life for growth. Here's what I mean. I've heard men preach who have said things like the following: "If you think you can smoke, and drink, and go to the movies and still go to Heaven, you're sadly mistaken!" These men are making salvation hinge upon man's good works. According to such men, how would you recognize a Christian? By what he believes or by Whom he is trusting? No, not at all, but rather by how he behaves.

I've known wonderful unbelievers who were better

behaved than a lot of Christians. Does that mean they are saved? Certainly not! When I received Christ as my Savior, there were several areas of my life that were not what they should have been, but I was still saved and growing. The Lord began to impress upon me that I was His and should honor Him in my life.

When I trusted Christ as my Savior I was smoking two and a half packs of cigarettes a day. Six months after I was saved I entered Bible school. I was still smoking and I was still saved. It took me more than a year of trying, by God's grace, to overcome the habit and to finally get it out of my life. I was saved although I was smoking, but at the same time I was growing. The Holy Spirit convicted me that my body was His temple and that I should not defile it.

God worked in my life and brought about this change and growth. Does that mean I'm now perfect? No, it only means that in a particular area of my life I've known something of growth, and I have the victory over that habit. There are many other areas of my life that still need improvement. Therefore, I am still growing and will need to continue growing until I meet the Lord face to face. God does work in His children's lives to bring about change and growth but this change comes at different rates for different people.

As I learned truths from God's Word and responded to them I began to grow. But suppose for a moment that one of these preachers that I described earlier had met me during those early days of my Christian life. Perhaps he would have seen me carrying my Bible to church while puffing on a cigarette. His erroneous conclusion would have been, "That guy is a hypocrite! He's pretending to be a Christian but the very fact that he's smoking proves that he's not." Often people like this focus on judging whether or not other people are saved by observing their behavior.

Because of this thing that we call "growth," it is not right or Scriptural to try to determine whether a person is saved based upon the level of his spiritual life. Let's consider two verses we previously looked at:

> For the grace of God that brings salvation has appeared to all men, teaching us that, denying ungodliness and worldly lusts, we should live soberly, righteously, and godly, in the present age.
>
> Titus 2:11–12

Notice what Titus says: "The grace of God...teaching us." And what does it teach us? Sometimes I hear men say that salvation, as I teach it, is nothing more than "cheap grace." I don't understand such reasoning. Grace is God's love in action. There's nothing cheap about that. Again this passage in Titus says, "The grace of God...teaching us." Does it teach us to live in sin? To do as we please? To live it up because we're saved and we can't lose it? Not at all. It teaches us to "deny ungodliness and worldly lusts, [and to] live soberly, righteously, and godly, in this present world." Isn't it clear from Titus 2:11–12 that salvation by God's grace is anything but "cheap" or dangerous? If it still does not seem clear then think on this verse, "For sin shall not have dominion over you, for you are not under law but under grace" (Romans 6:14). Why will sin not have dominion over the believer? Is it because he has a bunch of rules to follow? Is it because he'll be cast into hell if he doesn't forsake sin? No, no, a thousand times no! It is because he is under grace. Thank God He does not give us what we deserve!

I'm reminded of a story I heard one time about an "old battle-ax" who was quite unattractive. She had her photograph taken, and when she went back to the photographer to look at the proofs she went into a rage. She screamed, she fussed, she fumed, and she said she wouldn't pay the photographer anything. Just before she stomped out of the photo studio she screamed, "Why, not a single one of those photographs do me justice!" The meek, little photographer quietly, but firmly replied, "Lady, you don't need justice, you need mercy!" I don't know about you, but I need mercy. I don't want what I deserve.

It's wrong to set up our own standards of morality or ethics, and then preach that only those who measure up to them are really saved. That is self-righteous hypocrisy. Instead, recognize the Bible teaches that salvation is solely by faith, through God's grace, and recognize that a Christian is kept saved, is taught, and grows by that same grace. Once you weed out of your thinking the idea that human merit is a requirement for salvation, you will begin to understand that the Christian life is lived by grace and you will appreciate it as never before.

We do sin after we're saved. Even the beloved apostle John said, "If we say that we have [present tense] no sin, we deceive ourselves, and the truth is not in us" (1 John 1:8). Does that mean we lose our salvation every time we sin; or every time we commit a certain percentage of sins? Does it mean that because we do sin we should glory in it? Certainly not! Both extremes are just that—unscriptural extremes to be avoided at all cost.

The Scriptural attitude, therefore, should be that I am a sinner. Christ died for sinners (Romans 5:6). God loves me even while I am a sinner (Romans 5:8). He justifies (declares righteous) ungodly sinners who believe in Christ (Romans 4:5).

What About Backsliders, Hypocrites, and Apostates?

Who or what are backsliders, hypocrites, and apostates? Are they Christians or unbelievers? How can you know if you fall into one of these categories? Read on to discover the Bible's description of each and why it's important to know the differences between them. The purpose is to establish from Scripture whether these three classes of people are saved or lost, or whether they are lost people who at one time had been saved.

Backsliders

Some people suggest that although a person is a Christian when he trusts in the Lord, if he backslides he will lose his salvation. Backsliders are those who progress in their Christian growth and then through carelessness decline in their spiritual walk. What is the truth about backsliders according to the Bible?

The first thing that must be established is that only believers can backslide. The second important thing to note is that when God's children do backslide they are still God's children. And the third thing we find out from Scripture is that backsliding results not only in reaping what has been sown, but also being corrected by the backsliding itself. In Jeremiah 3:14 God says the following to Israel:

> Return, O backsliding children, says the Lord; for I am married to you. I will take you, one from a city and two from a family, and I will bring you to Zion.

Notice that these backsliders are "children," and God says—while they are in their backslidden condition—"I am married to you." Were they God's children? Yes, they were. God says so. Were they backsliders at the same time? Certainly.

You may ask, "If a believer can backslide and still be saved, then why wouldn't that lead to living a more sinful life?" There is a twofold reason it would not lead to that.

First, Proverbs 14:14 promises: "The backslider in heart will be filled with his own ways." Paul says the same thing in Galatians 6:7: "Do not be deceived, God is not mocked; for whatever a man sows, that will he also reap." In other words, backsliding makes one absolutely miserable. He will reap the very thing he is doing. God often uses this misery to nudge His child back to His ways.

Second, God says in Jeremiah 2:19: "Your own wickedness will correct you, and your backslidings will rebuke you..." You see, a disobedient child of God has God's chastening hand upon him, plus the Holy Spirit convicting him from within. This simply establishes the truth about which we have already written, that a genuine believer in Christ cannot live as he pleases and get by with it without consequences. God does not just leave us to ourselves, but uses all things in our lives to drive us to Himself.

Hypocrites

Woe to you, scribes and Pharisees, hypocrites! For you are like whitewashed tombs which indeed appear beautiful outwardly, but inside are full of dead men's bones and all uncleanness. Even so you also outwardly appear righteous to men, but inside you are full of hypocrisy and lawlessness.

Matthew 23:27–28

If a person is a hypocrite, then he must, by definition, be acting falsely. A hypocrite pretends to be one thing while in reality he is something else. Christians are sometimes hypocritical by pretending to be spiritual outwardly while inwardly they are not, but when the Lord Jesus Christ condemned the hypocrites (as in Matthew 23), he condemned unbelievers who were pretending to be believers.

He not only called them hypocrites; He also said they were "sons of hell" (verse 15), "blind guides" (verse 16), "fools and blind" (verses 17 and 18), and "serpents and brood of vipers" (verse 33). He also said that these hypocrites only cleaned up the outside of themselves, but not the inside (verses 25 and 26). Jesus said that these men appeared to be spiritually alive, but were in reality, spiritually dead (verse 27). They appeared to be righteous while actually they were full of lawlessness (verse 28). They gave honor to the dead prophets, but Jesus said that had they lived at the time of the prophets these Pharisees would have killed them (verses 29–31). Finally, in clear, stinging language, Jesus let them know that there was no way for them to "escape the condemnation of hell" (verse 33).

Luke further elaborates upon Jesus' condemnation of these religious leaders.

> Woe to you, scribes and Pharisees, hypocrites! For you are like graves which are not seen, and the men who walk over them are not aware of them.
>
> Luke 11:44

> Woe to you! For you build the tombs of the prophets, and your fathers killed them. In fact, you bear witness that you approve the deeds of your fathers; for they indeed killed them, and you build their tombs. Therefore the wisdom of God also said, I will send them prophets and apostles, and some of them they will kill and persecute.
>
> Luke 11:47–49

Notice the phrase in verse 48: "In fact, you bear witness that you approve the deeds of your fathers; for they indeed killed them (the prophets), and you build their tombs." There is no doubt that Jesus was exposing and condemning these religious leaders who deceived others into thinking they were pious.

There are many religious leaders and people today who are hypocrites. They play the part just like the Pharisees did in Bible times. They work at having the outward appearance of being devout and God-fearing. They talk using Christian terms and they become part of Christian groups, but they are not believers. They are hypocrites, pretending to be Christian in order to gain what is important to them, such as power, influence or wealth.

First John 2:18–19 describes people who pretend to be saved or to believe certain doctrines when, in reality they do not.

> Little children, it is the last hour; and as you have heard that Antichrist is coming, even now many antichrists have come, by which we know that it is the last hour. They went out from us, but they were not of us; for if they had been of us, they would have continued with us; but they went out that they might be made manifest, that none of them were of us.

Notice that the people referred to are called "antichrists." They always have been antichrists, even while they were identified with, and recognized as one of the believers. And John says clearly, "They went out from us...that they might be made manifest that none of them were of us." More literally that last phrase would read, "that they were not at all of us." In other words, although they appeared to be one of the sheep, the whole time they were among the sheep but not of the sheep. In light of the Scriptures, therefore, we ought not to classify hypocrites with believers, but recognize that hypocrites are pretenders—false actors, and not the genuine article at all.

Apostates

When speaking of salvation, apostates, like hypocrites, are never saved in the first place. To apostatize—when used in a religious sense—usually means to depart from previously held truth. But it is important to note that a person may give mental assent to many truths regarding Jesus Christ, and yet never really trust Him. Therefore, when someone apostatizes they are departing from previously held persuasions.

I have found that, by far, the greatest number of so-called apostates come from church backgrounds that teach works are necessary for salvation. Here, for instance, is a familiar old story. Tim goes to church faithfully. He believes "with all his heart." He is told—and he has no reason to doubt it—that he must believe in the Lord, obey Him, pray through, endure to the end, speak in tongues, keep the Law, etc. After years of faithfully trying to do all the many things that he has been told he must do in order to go to Heaven, he finally gives up in despair. He honestly faces the fact that he cannot keep from failing. His despair leads to being critical of those in church who are still pretending to be righteous when he knows they are not. His critical attitude turns to scorn of all those "hypocrites." His scorn turns to downright antagonistic opposition. His former friends in the church begin to talk about him this way, "Pray for poor brother Tim. He has backslidden so much that he has become an apostate."

If I were talking to any of the members of such a church, I can hear now what they'd say: "You can't tell me that all you have to do to go to Heaven is believe in Christ. That's not enough. Why, I have a friend named Tim who used to believe in the Lord and today he's a complete apostate—denies the faith, attacks the Bible and laughs at Christians. You mean to tell me he's still saved just because he believed at one time?"

The truth of the matter is that there are thousands upon thousands of "Tims" who have never really trusted the Lord Jesus Christ alone for their salvation. Oh, they used to believe many Biblical doctrines about Him; they may have had many wonderful religious "experiences;" but they were also depending upon their own goodness and works to get to Heaven. According to Scripture men who depend upon any effort of their own for their salvation are not really saved at all. What they need to understand and believe is the true and simple Gospel of God's grace.

At one time, during my high school years, I was what might be termed an apostate. I tried to go along with what my church had told me, but I just couldn't seem to do it. So, I finally gave up trying. I thought I had turned my back upon God. The truth of the matter is I turned my back upon a counterfeit of the Gospel—a Christian "system." I hadn't turned my back upon Christ (though I thought I had), but I had refused the idea of Christ that had been portrayed to me by so-called Christian people. When I stopped going to church, and later in high school even mocked the whole thing, I could have been classified as an apostate—one who "used to believe but doesn't any more."

The second chapter of 2 Peter is often used to try to prove that apostates are people who used to be saved and are now lost.

> For if, after they have escaped the pollutions of the world through the knowledge of the Lord and Saviour Jesus Christ, they are again entangled in them and overcome, the latter end is worse for them than the beginning.
>
> 2 Peter 2:20

But 2 Peter points out clearly that the "apostates" of this chapter are men who only had knowledge of Christ and salvation, but never knew Him personally. For instance, in verse one they are quite clearly called "false teachers." If they are false teachers, then they can't be true teachers. These apostates are said to "speak evil of the things that they do not understand" (2 Peter 2:12). They do not really understand the genuine Gospel, and so they begin speaking evil of what they call the gospel, which is not the real Gospel at all. They are also called "dogs" and "sows." God's children are never called either. Genuine believers are called sheep.

Second Peter 2:21 goes on to say about these false teachers:

> It would have been better for them not to have known the way of righteousness, than having known it, to turn from the holy commandment delivered to them.

This perfectly describes what apostates do. They "have known the way of righteousness," which is entirely different than knowing Christ personally. They understand a lot about righteous ways but do not know the Savior. They apply Christian principles to their morality and this helps them in their personal lives but they are not saved. What did they do after knowing and using these principles? They "turned from them" and are worse off than before. Notice, it does not say that they turned from *Him*; they turned from *it*—the "holy commandment." Many who are now skeptics and atheists have in the past lived by some divine principles which they now reject. However, knowledge of God and knowing Him are entirely different.

Are there apostates in the world? Yes, indeed. Were they once saved but now lost? Not at all. They temporarily believed certain Christian doctrines which they later denied. That is entirely different from knowing Christ personally as your Savior. Apostates do not know Him, nor have they ever known Him.

There are those who have reached other erroneous conclusions concerning the security of the believer in Christ, basing their interpretations on Bible verses taken out of context. It is so important to clarify these misunderstandings that in the next chapter I will explain these verses within their various contexts.

Important Passages
to Examine

There are more than a few passages in Scripture that—at first glance—seem to indicate that a truly saved person may end up losing his or her salvation if certain conditions are not met. Though these verses may cause anxiety to the sincere student of the Bible, a close examination of the contents of each passage, and its surrounding context, will quickly dispel any misunderstandings. With total confidence that the Scriptures are not contradictory in any way, we will now examine a number of these sometimes puzzling portions of the Bible.

Matthew 7:13–14

"Enter by the narrow gate; for wide is the gate and broad is the way that leads to destruction, and there are many who go in by it. Because narrow is the gate and difficult is the way which leads to life, and there are few who find it."

The assumption that is sometimes drawn from these two verses is that the "narrow way" and the "straight gate" represent a strict path that leads to Heaven. The path usually represents a holy life. If you walk on that narrow way—and are careful not to step off of it—you'll eventually be saved. Of course, if you step off that narrow path you lose your salvation.

It's amazing how much can be read into a passage of Scripture when we allow our imaginations to run wild. But when we carefully compare Scripture with Scripture such erroneous interpretations do not develop. For instance, Jesus said in John 10:9 that "I am the door. If anyone enters by Me, he will be saved, and will go in and out and find pasture." So the gate or door we must enter is Christ Himself. He is a straight gate because He is the only entrance into God's Heaven—there is no other way. In fact Jesus developed this same thought even further in John 10:1: "Most assuredly, I say to you, he who does not enter the sheepfold by the door, but climbs up some other way, the same is a thief and a robber."

The "narrow way" that leads to life is also the Lord Jesus Christ, as we see in John 14:6 "Jesus said to him, 'I am the way, the truth, and the life. No one comes to the Father except through Me.'" In both instances Christ is the gate and the way. Therefore, He is the straight gate and the narrow way, because there is no other gate to Heaven, nor any other way.

Matthew 7:13–14, therefore, has nothing whatever to do with one's behavior or losing salvation.

Matthew 8:12

"But the sons of the kingdom will be cast out into outer darkness. There will be weeping and gnashing of teeth."

We are sometimes told that since the "sons of the kingdom" shall be cast into outer darkness, this is proof positive that children of God may lose their salvation. Again, we need to emphasize the importance of keeping a statement in context, and in harmony with the rest of Scripture. In Matthew 8:5 a Gentile centurion came to Christ desirous of having his servant healed. And he told the Lord that all He would have to do would be to speak the word and his servant would be healed. Then the Scripture records, "When Jesus heard it, He marveled, and said to those who followed, 'Assuredly, I say to you, I have not found such great faith, not even in Israel!'" (Matthew 8:10).

Christ is obviously saying that many Gentiles ("many shall come from the east and west") will believe and be with Abraham, Isaac, and Jacob in the kingdom. On the other hand, verse 12 points out that many of the "sons of the kingdom" (Jews to whom the kingdom was promised) will be cast into outer darkness. It is just another way of saying many Gentiles will be saved and many Jews won't.

Being a child of the kingdom is not the same as being a child of God, for we have recorded in Revelation 20:3 and 20:7–15 that many of the people of the nations who will be

living during Christ's earthly kingdom will follow Satan
in his rebellion against the Lord Jesus Christ. During the
Kingdom people will be raising families and reproducing as
they do now. Each person will be responsible to trust Christ
as people are responsible to do at the present time. Just
living in the kingdom will be no guarantee at all that they
belong to the Lord.

Matthew 10:22

*"And you will be hated by all for My name's sake. But he
who endures to the end will be saved."*

In this chapter Christ is giving His 12 disciples
instructions as to what they will do as they go forth to
preach. Starting in verse 16 He especially begins to warn the
disciples about men—especially men's attempts to destroy
their preaching and testimony. He tells them that they will
be like "sheep in the midst of wolves" (verse 16); He says,
"beware of men" (verse 17); He tells them that men "will
deliver you up to the councils, and they will scourge you
in their synagogues" (verse 17); He informs them that "you
will be brought before governors and kings for My sake,
as a testimony to them and to the Gentiles" (verse 18); He
even warns them of the fact that "brother will deliver up
brother to death, and a father his child; and children will
rise up against parents and cause them to be put to death"

(verse 21); lastly, He warns them that "you will be hated by all for My name's sake" (verse 22).

After all of this warning regarding what men will do to them He tells them, "But he who endures to the end will be saved." In order to understand this statement we must answer in our own minds two very important questions. First, what is it that is to be endured; and secondly, from what shall the one who endures be saved?[13]

I think it becomes immediately obvious that enduring refers to enduring the attempts of men to silence their witness. And the promise is that if the disciples would endure all of the attempts of men to silence them—that is, if they did not give in to the pressures of the enemies of the Gospel—they would be saved from those very men and their attempts to keep the disciples quiet. You may say to yourself, "Well, if that's the meaning of it, He didn't have to say it. It's obvious if I endure men's persecutions I'll be saved from them." No, it isn't obvious. Put yourself in the place of the disciples. They were being sent out for the first time to preach for Christ. Some of them could well have had the question in their mind, "What should I do if I'm opposed, or if men persecute me?" It's only human to try to figure out what to do in such circumstances. Christ solved the question for them. In effect He said, "I will deliver you on one condition—that you don't give in." The deliverance, of course, had to do with deliverance from physical violence—

not eternal salvation.

When Christ sent out His 12 disciples in Matthew 10, He promised them deliverance from their persecutors if they stood firm. They did stand firm and all 12 returned later to give their reports of the results of their preaching journey. However, later on when 11 of these 12 (Judas not included) began preaching the Gospel they were all martyred for the faith with the possible exception of John, who died in exile. Christ had given them no promise of deliverance that last time.

Matthew 16:24–26

"Then Jesus said to His disciples, 'If anyone desires to come after Me, let him deny himself, and take up his cross, and follow Me. For whoever desires to save his life will lose it, but whoever loses his life for My sake will find it. For what profit is it to a man if he gains the whole world, and loses his own soul? Or what will a man give in exchange for his soul?' "

There is a vast difference between telling an unbeliever to come to Christ for salvation, and telling a man who is already saved to come after Christ for service. Coming to Christ (salvation) deals with the future life, while coming after Christ (service) has to do with the present life here on earth—the Christian's life.

Notice to whom Christ is speaking in verse 24—"His

disciples." These are men who are already saved and it is to them that He said, "If any man will come after me, let him deny himself, and take up his cross, and follow me." They had already come to Him and now were invited to come after Him.

The only real reason that anyone ever uses Matthew 16:24–26 to try to prove the possibility of losing one's salvation is the use of the word "soul" in verse 26. "For what profit is it to a man if he gains the whole world, and loses his own soul? Or what will a man give in exchange for his soul?" Those who believe a saved man can lose his salvation point out that the implication of these verses is that if you don't deny yourself, and take up your cross, that you'll lose your own soul (which, to them, means you'll lose your salvation). However, all confusion about the matter is immediately cleared up when you realize that the word "life" (used twice in verse 25) and the word "soul" (used twice in verse 26) come from the same word in the Greek and should be translated "life" every time. For example, the American Standard Version translates it, "what shall a man give in exchange for his life"; Goodspeed translates it, "if he gains the whole world at the cost of his life"; and the New English Bible translates it, "if he shall gain the whole world at the cost of his true self."

Not only does the definition of the Greek word bear out the fact that the present life is in view in this passage, but the context itself does also. As we mentioned before, Christ is speaking to those already saved, and inviting them to live for Him now. The crux of the whole matter is in verse 25, where Christ gives this promise, "For whoever desires to save his life will lose it, but whoever loses his life for My sake will find it."

Matthew 25:1–10

"Then the kingdom of heaven shall be likened to ten virgins who took their lamps and went out to meet the bridegroom. Now five of them were wise, and five were foolish. Those who were foolish took their lamps and took no oil with them, but the wise took oil in their vessels with their lamps. But while the bridegroom was delayed, they all slumbered and slept. And at midnight a cry was heard: 'Behold, the bridegroom is coming; go out to meet him!' Then all those virgins arose and trimmed their lamps. And the foolish said to the wise, 'Give us some of your oil, for our lamps are going out.' But the wise answered, saying, 'No, lest there should not be enough for us and you; but go rather to those who sell, and buy for yourselves.' And while they went to buy, the bridegroom came, and those who were ready went in with him to the wedding; and the door was shut."

There is one point to the parable of the ten virgins. It is found in verse 13 "Watch therefore, for you know neither the day nor the hour in which the Son of Man is coming." I think it is foolish to try to identify the five foolish virgins, the five wise virgins, the lamps, the oil, the midnight hour, etc. The details of the parable are not the important thing; the point of the parable is important. And the point is that we'd better be alert, for the Lord could come back at any time.

However, there are those who dogmatically identify all the points of the parable, even though Christ himself did not bother to identify those same points. Some of these well-meaning people tell us the five foolish virgins were five Christians who lost their salvation because they didn't watch. We are told that oil is a type of the Holy Spirit in this passage, and because the five foolish virgins burned up their oil (lost the Holy Spirit), they lost their salvation. Well, if the five foolish virgins were unsaved at any time, they were unsaved all the time, for you read in verse 3 that they "took no oil with them." It doesn't say they lost their oil, or burned up their oil; they simply didn't have any. When they went to buy oil for their lamps the bridegroom came. They bought oil and returned to the door of the marriage feast; when they knocked for entrance the bridegroom said, "I know you not." So, if oil is a type of the Holy Spirit, then when they came back to the door to enter the marriage feast, they would have been saved because they had oil (The Holy Spirit). But the bridegroom said, "I know you not." He shouldn't have said that to them if oil is a type of the Holy Spirit, and they had the Holy Spirit. Do you see how ridiculous all of this becomes? The bridegroom came—those who were ready went in with him to the marriage feast—those who were not ready did not enter in because He did not know them. The same will be true when Christ returns. Those who know Him (and are, therefore, ready) will go with Him. Those who do not know Him (and are, therefore, not ready) will not go with Him. It is as simple as that, and has nothing to do with losing one's salvation.

Luke 9:62

"But Jesus said to him, 'No one, having put his hand to the plow, and looking back, is fit for the kingdom of God.' "

The subject matter of this passage, as in previous passages we've considered, is the present life not the future life; working for the Lord now, not gaining salvation in the future. We see this in verse 56 where Christ said, "For the Son of Man did not come to destroy men's lives but to save them. And they went to another village." The very next verse, a man said to Christ, "Lord, I will follow You wherever You go." He replied to this man that even though the foxes have holes, and the birds have nests that He (the Son of man) didn't even have a place to lay His head. Then, in verse 59, Christ said to another man, "Follow Me." But he said, "Lord, let me first go and bury my father." Christ rebuked him with the words, "Let the dead bury their own dead, but you go and preach the kingdom of God." Then another man came along and said, "Lord, I will follow You, but let me first go and bid them farewell who are at my house." And it is to this man that Jesus said, "No one, having put his hand to the plow, and looking back, is fit for the kingdom of God."

I repeat, the subject matter is following Christ, not receiving Him as Savior. The word "fit" in verse 62 actually means "well-placed" and has to do with having a place of honor in the kingdom. The question in view is not whether a man who puts his hand to the plough and looks back will be in the kingdom, but rather, if such a man will have an honorable place in the kingdom. The Williams Translation brings this out so beautifully when he translates it the following way: "Jesus said to him, no man who puts his hand to the plough, and then continues to look back, is fitted for service in the kingdom of God."

Service is, after all, what the passage is about. Remember, the Son of man, came to save lives, and a Christian man's life can only be saved as he loses it for Christ's sake—as he follows Christ without looking back. Such a man will be honored by the Lord. Jesus points this out so well in John 12:26: "If anyone serves Me, let him follow Me; and where I am, there My servant will be also. If anyone serves Me, him My Father will honor."

Luke 12:42–46

"And the Lord said, 'Who then is that faithful and wise steward, whom his master will make ruler over his household, to give them their portion of food in due season? Blessed is that servant whom his master will find so doing when he comes. Truly, I say to you that he will make him ruler over all that he has. But if that servant says in his heart, "My master is delaying his coming," and begins to beat the male and female servants, and to eat and drink and be drunk, the master of that servant will come on a day when he is not looking for him, and at an hour when he is not aware, and will cut him in two and appoint him his portion with the unbelievers.' "

The reason some think that this passage teaches we can lose our salvation is the statement made in verse 46 that the unfaithful servant will be cut in two and the lord will "appoint him his portion with the unbelievers." If you have a good reference Bible (that is, one with good cross references and gives the meaning of words), you'll notice that the word "unbelievers" ought to read "unfaithful." This, of course, is in complete harmony with the passage itself. The question is asked in verse 42, "Who then is that faithful and wise steward, whom his master will make ruler over his household, to give them their portion of food in due season?" God then describes that "faithful and wise steward." In verse 45 He describes the unfaithful and unwise steward. This is the point of the parable. If you're faithful and wise you'll be ruler over all that the Lord has (verse 44). On the other hand, if you're unfaithful and you're unwise, you'll have your portion with the unfaithful.

The unwise and unfaithful servant is like the man described in 1 Corinthians 3, who, although he is built upon the foundation of Christ (verses 11–12), yet all of his works are burned up so that he suffers loss (verse 15). But the Scripture says that "he himself shall be saved; yet so as through fire." This man is an unfaithful servant who loses his reward; but, notice, he is still saved.

The same is true of the servant in Luke 12. He thinks the coming of the Lord has been delayed. Therefore, he behaves in an unwise and unfaithful manner. When the Lord returns He will deal with this unfaithful servant severely. However, this unfaithful servant still belongs to the Lord as it is clearly stated in verse 46 "the master of that servant will come on a day when he is not looking for him."

John 8:31

"Then Jesus said to those Jews who believed Him, 'If you abide in My word, you are My disciples indeed.' "

To obtain a better picture of what Christ is speaking of in verse 31, I think we need to go back to His statement in verse 29, "And He who sent Me is with Me. The Father has not left Me alone, for I always do those things that please Him." These are terrific words proving beyond any question that Jesus Christ has to be God in the flesh. For no mere man can always do what pleases the Father. Christ, however, did please the Father all the time. When the people heard this statement by Christ it is recorded in verse 30 that "many believed in Him." In other words, they were saved because God guarantees in Acts 16:31, "Believe on the Lord Jesus Christ, and you will be saved." Christ bears this out in verse 31 where we read, "Then Jesus said to those Jews who believed Him, 'If you abide in My word, you are My disciples indeed.'" He is not telling unbelievers how to become believers, or telling the ungodly how to become godly, or telling those who are going to hell how to go to Heaven. He is telling those who have just trusted Him how they may become disciples of His. You see, the word disciple means "a learner." It is one thing to trust Him for your salvation. It is another thing to be taught by Him, to learn from Him, and to follow Him in service. This is what Christ is promising them in verse 31—not salvation. He said to those who believed on Him, "If you abide in My word, you are My disciples indeed." Unbelievers become believers by trusting Christ. Believers become disciples by continuing in His word. There is no thought at all in this passage of obtaining salvation, keeping salvation, or losing salvation.

John 10:27–28

"My sheep hear My voice, and I know them, and they follow Me. And I give them eternal life, and they shall never perish; neither shall anyone snatch them out of My hand."

You may be surprised that I'm including this verse among those that are used to teach that a person can lose his salvation. Generally this verse is used to support just the opposite view, that once a man is saved he can "never perish." I include it here because an entire doctrine is built upon one word, and it needs clarification. That one word is "follow" in verse 27. The logic runs this way: There is only one kind of person who shall never perish: he who hears Christ's voice and follows Christ. By following Christ these people usually mean that it is necessary to obey Christ in every detail of our lives. When we do that, they reason, we are "following." And as long as we follow we shall never perish.

However, this interpretation of the word "follow" is completely inadmissible in context. Christ is not referring to how much we obey Him; He is concerned with whether we follow Him or someone else—the "stranger" of verse 5. Notice what Jesus says about following:

> Yet they will by no means follow a stranger, but will flee from him, for they do not know the voice of strangers. Jesus used this illustration, but they did not understand the things which He spoke

to them. Then Jesus said to them again, Most assuredly, I say to you, I am the door of the sheep. All who ever came before Me are thieves and robbers, but the sheep did not hear them.

John 10:5–8

Every believer in Christ "follows" Christ in the way that this word is used in this chapter. In other words, we are not following Sun Myung Moon, Mary Baker Eddy, or the Dalai Lama—we are following Christ. We are following Him to Heaven. Jesus said, "I go to prepare a place for you. And if I go and prepare a place for you, I will come again and receive you to Myself; that where I am, there you may be also" (John 14:2–3).

So, it can be said that John 10:27–28 does teach the security of the believer, because all believers are followers of Christ rather than followers of someone else.

John 15:1–6

"I am the true vine, and My Father is the vinedresser. Every branch in Me that does not bear fruit He takes away; and every branch that bears fruit He prunes, that it may bear more fruit. You are already clean because of the word which I have spoken to you. Abide in Me, and I in you. As the branch cannot bear fruit of itself, unless it abides in the vine, neither can you, unless you abide in Me. I am the vine, you are the branches. He who abides in Me, and I in him,

bears much fruit; for without Me you can do nothing. If anyone does not abide in Me, he is cast out as a branch and is withered; and they gather them and throw them into the fire, and they are burned."

The phrase in this passage that leads men to believe that this is referring to a Christian who has lost his salvation is the phrase found in verse 6. "If anyone does not abide in Me, he is cast out as a branch and is withered; and they gather them and throw them into the fire, and they are burned." There are several flaws in assuming that this verse teaches that a believer who does not remain faithful is put into hell.

First, it is not God who cast these people into the fire. It is men. Read it carefully in your own Bible—"they gather them and throw them into the fire, and they are burned." The word "they" refers to men as clearly translated in the King James Bible: "men gather them."

Second, it doesn't say they are cast into hell. Men cannot cast other men into hell. It only says they are cast into the fire. A good cross reference for this is Luke 6:22, "Blessed are you when men hate you, and when they exclude you, and revile you, and cast out your name as evil, for the Son of Man's sake." Men can do that, but they cannot cast a believer into hell.

Third, the branch in verse 6 is not a literal branch—it is a believer. Christ pointed this out in verse 5 when He said, "I am the vine, you are the branches." By the same token the fire may not be a literal fire. For instance, there is the fire of persecution when we stand for the Lord and men revile us for our faith; there is the fire of ridicule (which I think is spoken of here) that we may receive from men when they know that we are Christians, and yet our lives are not consistent with our profession.

In any case, there is no hint in this passage that God is taking this unfruitful branch and throwing it into hell. In addition, Jesus is speaking to His 11 disciples (believers) about bearing fruit, not about remaining saved. Fruit bearing is the subject, not salvation.

1 Corinthians 9:27

"But I discipline my body and bring it into subjection, lest, when I have preached to others, I myself should become disqualified."

It is true that Paul preached in such a way that when he was through preaching to others he himself would not be disqualified. The question is disqualified from what? The illustration given in the passage from verse 24 to the end of the chapter is of an athletic contest. Many run in the contest, but only one receives the prize. The ones who do not receive the prize are the losers. They run just as the winner runs, but the winner wins the prize, the losers do not. So, Paul says in the verse that he brings his body into subjection so that he won't be disqualified. Disqualified from what?—disqualified from the race. The race for what?—the race for the prize (verse 24), the race for the crown (verse 25). Not the race for eternal life. Eternal life is never said to be a prize or a crown that we earn. The Bible says eternal life is God's gift. "For the wages of sin is death, but the gift of God is eternal life in Christ Jesus our Lord" (Romans 6:23). "For by grace you have been saved through faith, and that not of yourselves; it is the gift of God, not of works, lest anyone should boast" (Ephesians 2:8–9). Salvation, or eternal life, is always portrayed in Scripture as a free gift God gives those who trust Christ. It is never illustrated as a prize that we win by effort or work. In fact just the opposite is true.

If someone interprets 1 Corinthians 9:27 as proof that we must strive and work and put ourselves under subjection to gain eternal life, that same person has to completely ignore more than 150 verses which teach that salvation is received simply by faith (listed in Appendix B).

Moreover, the word disqualified literally means disapproved. This, again, bears out the thought that they are disapproved for the prize—the crown—not disapproved for salvation. The opposite of being disapproved is being approved, and God tells His children how to be approved in 2 Timothy 2:15: "Be diligent to present yourself approved to God, a worker who does not need to be ashamed, rightly dividing the word of truth." God has two kinds of children:

those who are good workmen and those who aren't. A good workman is approved. A poor workman is not. A good workman receives a prize. A poor workman doesn't. A good workman receives a crown. A poor workman does not. They both have eternal life and are saved. In the same chapter of 2 Timothy this is also pointed out in verse 20: "But in a great house there are not only vessels of gold and silver, but also of wood and clay, some for honor and some for dishonor." But notice, both kinds of vessels are in the house—in this case, God's house. All Christians are also in the race for the prize. This is stated in 1 Corinthians 9:24, "Do you not know that those who run in a race all run, but one receives the prize? Run in such a way that you may obtain it." Another way of saying it would be that in a race all the runners compete—all of them run, but only the winner receives the prize. It is so important to clearly divide Scripture into passages on salvation and passages on service. Failure to do this leads to unbelievable confusion.

Galatians 5:19–21

"Now the works of the flesh are evident, which are: adultery, fornication, uncleanness, lewdness, idolatry, sorcery, hatred, contentions, jealousies, outbursts of wrath, selfish ambitions, dissensions, heresies, envy, murders, drunkenness, revelries, and the like; of which I tell you

beforehand, just as I also told you in time past, that those who practice such things will not inherit the kingdom of God."

What are these sins described in these three verses? Verse 19 says they are "the works of the flesh." And verse 21 concludes that "those who practice such things [the works of the flesh] will not inherit the kingdom of God." This is in perfect harmony with all of Scripture. For instance, in 1 Corinthians 15:50 we read, "Now this I say, brethren, that flesh and blood cannot inherit the kingdom of God; nor does corruption inherit incorruption." Those in the flesh cannot inherit the kingdom of God because the flesh is corrupt. This corrupt flesh must put on incorruption. This is further developed in 1 Corinthians 15:53, "For this corruptible must put on incorruption, and this mortal must put on immortality." This "corruptible" is the flesh, and this "mortal" is the flesh. Flesh and blood cannot inherit the kingdom of God. We need a new birth—a birth of the Spirit—to inherit God's kingdom.

Paul spoke of the same thing in 1 Corinthians 6:9–11:

> Do you not know that the unrighteous will not inherit the kingdom of God? Do not be deceived. Neither fornicators, nor idolaters, nor adulterers, nor homosexuals, nor sodomites, nor thieves, nor covetous, nor drunkards, nor revilers, nor extortioners will inherit the kingdom of God. And such were some of you. But you were washed, but you were sanctified, but you were justified in the name of the Lord Jesus and by the Spirit of our God.

It is not true that anyone who is guilty of any of these things is automatically excluded from Heaven. It is not true that a liar cannot go to Heaven. It is not true that an idolater cannot go to Heaven. It is not true that a thief, or a drunkard, or an adulterer cannot go to Heaven. What is true is that any sinner—anyone who does the deeds of the flesh—who has not been washed, sanctified, or justified in the name of the Lord Jesus (verse 11) cannot inherit the kingdom of God. Paul was a murderer, but that didn't keep him from being saved. When Saul the murderer trusted Jesus Christ he was washed and cleansed, justified by faith and was on his way to Heaven. The same could be said of men like David, and Moses, and Lot. Every one of them was a sinner—just as we are—and because flesh and blood cannot enter the kingdom of God, they needed—and we need—a new birth from God. This new birth (the birth of the Spirit) is what enters the kingdom of God—not our old sinful flesh. The very fact that those who commit "the works of the flesh" are not qualified for the kingdom of God is proof positive that such people—which includes all the world—need God's salvation, and need it desperately. This is why God offers it freely instead of telling us to work for it, because our flesh leads to the kind of works described in Galatians 5:19–21. We need a Spirit-birth that qualifies us for entrance into God's holy kingdom. God gladly gives this to those who trust in His Son. "And this is the testimony: that God has given us eternal life, and this life is in His Son. He who has the Son has life; he who does not have the Son of God does not have life" (1 John 5:11–12).

Philippians 2:12

"Therefore, my beloved, as you have always obeyed, not as in my presence only, but now much more in my absence, work out your own salvation with fear and trembling."

The apostle Paul is writing from prison to those whom he had led to Christ. He reminds them in this verse that when he had been with them they were obedient to the Lord. He urges them to be just as obedient in his absence as they were in his presence. Then he says, "Work out your own salvation with fear and trembling for [because] it is God who works in you both to will and to do for His good pleasure."

There are those who attempt to make verse 12 a command to work for salvation, but no matter how hard one may try, "out" cannot be made to mean "for." We are able to work out our salvation in our practical day-to-day lives because God is in us, working through us (verse 13). God only lives in the child of God, so these to whom Paul wrote these words were saved—they had God in them. The verses following verse 12 tell us where we are to work out our salvation, and how to do it. We are to work out our salvation "in the midst of a crooked and perverse generation" (verse 15). The way we are to do it is by "holding fast the word of life" (verse 16).

Working out your salvation would be the same as if I gave you a plot of land and I told you to "work it." If I give it to you, it's yours; but if you don't work it, it doesn't produce—weeds will grow. If you do work it, it will produce. The farthest thing from Paul's mind is the idea of working for his salvation.

Colossians 1:21–23

"And you, who once were alienated and enemies in your mind by wicked works, yet now He has reconciled in the body of His flesh through death, to present you holy, and blameless, and above reproach in His sight—if indeed you continue in the faith, grounded and steadfast, and are not moved away from the hope of the gospel which you heard, which was preached to every creature under heaven, of which I, Paul, became a minister."

This is one of the so-called "if" passages. It is often taught that there are many passages in the Bible where God says He will save someone "if" they meet certain conditions. Such conditions often vary so much that one would have to know the whole Bible to know what all the conditions are. That God would demand so many different things for salvation is unthinkable. Salvation would then depend upon knowledge of all these conditions instead of just simple faith in the person and work of Jesus Christ.

The "if" in Colossians 1:23 is supposed to be one of these conditions. The logic runs like this: God will save you if you continue in the faith. If you don't continue in the faith, you will not be presented before Him in Heaven. There are two things that are nearly always overlooked when someone interprets this passage in this way.

I think you will see what I'm talking about in the answers to the following two questions. First, consider the subject of verse 22. Is it *about* believers being presented before the Lord, or is it *how* we will be presented before the Lord? The passage does not say we will be presented before the Lord if we continue in the faith. It does say we will be presented in a certain way if we continue. Those who continue in the faith, "grounded and steadfast," and who are not moved away from the anticipation of the Gospel will be presented before the Lord a certain way. That way is "holy and blameless and above reproach in his sight."

All Christians are going to be presented, but not all Christians are going to be presented "holy, blameless and above reproach." What proof do I have for such a statement? 1 Thessalonians 3:12–13 says:

> And may the Lord make you increase and abound in love to one another and to all, just as we do to you, so that He may establish your

hearts blameless in holiness before our God and Father at the coming of our Lord Jesus Christ with all His saints.

According to Paul's words in this passage these to whom he is writing will be presented "blameless in holiness" if they "increase and abound in love." This is not salvation; this is service.

Notice 1 John 2:28: "And now, little children, abide in Him, that when He appears, we may have confidence and not be ashamed before Him at His coming." There are some believers who will have confidence and be unashamed before the Lord when He comes. There are others who will lack confidence and be ashamed. What will be the difference? The difference is, as 1 John puts it, "abiding in Him;" or as 1 Thessalonians words it, "abounding in love;" or as expressed in Colossians 1:23, "continuing in the faith, grounded and steadfast." All of these expressions talk about the same thing. In other words, from a personal standpoint, the issue involved in Colossians 1:21–23 is not whether I will be presented before the Lord. The real issue, instead, is, how I may be presented before Him in a blameless fashion.

One other thing that's often overlooked in this passage is that the condition for being presented before the Lord in a holy, blameless and above reproach way is not simply continuing in the faith. The condition is continuing in the faith "grounded and steadfast." Believers do continue in the faith, but not all believers continue in the faith "grounded and steadfast." What is being spoken of in verse 23 is spiritual growth or spiritual maturity. Those who grow in the faith become settled and grounded and stable. These are the ones who will be blameless and above reproach. Those who do not continue in the faith in this way will be, as 1 John points out, "ashamed before Him at his coming."

Another thing that disproves the idea that continuing in the faith is necessary to keep one's salvation is the context in which we find verse 23. For instance, in verse 20, God says that Christ has already made peace. He words it this way, "having made peace through the blood of His cross." God then adds in verse 21 the following clear statement: "And you, who once were alienated and enemies in your mind by wicked works, yet now He has reconciled." So, those to whom he is writing in verses 21–23 are those that Christ has already reconciled in verse 21, and has already given peace to in verse 20. What He is urging them to do now is to continue to be stable in their faith so that when the Lord returns and gives out rewards, these believers may be presented in a holy, blameless, and above reproach fashion.

2 Thessalonians 1:8

"In flaming fire taking vengeance on those who do not know God, and on those who do not obey the gospel of our Lord Jesus Christ."

Many infer from this verse that you must obey God in everything or Christ will come back and take vengeance upon you. However, this verse should not be viewed in this way. We need only to take the verse at face value to see that. Upon whom does God take vengeance? Upon those who obey not the Gospel. What is the Gospel? The Gospel is that Jesus Christ died for our sins, was buried, and came back from the dead to provide salvation for us (1 Corinthians 15:3–4). The Lord Jesus Christ gives eternal life to those who depend upon Him. That's the Gospel—the good news. Those who obey God regarding the Gospel do not have to worry about Him taking vengeance upon them. Those who don't obey God regarding the Gospel will have God's wrath poured out upon them. This is stated clearly in John 3:36: "He who believes in the Son has everlasting life; and he who does not believe the Son shall not see life, but the wrath of God abides on him."

It simply is not true that to escape God's wrath I must obey everything He says. If that were the case, there wouldn't be a person on the face of the earth who has lived, is living now, or ever will live, who could qualify for salvation. No, God's Gospel is the thing we are to obey. And the Gospel is that He gives eternal life freely to those who trust Him for it.

1 Timothy 4:16

"Take heed to yourself and to the doctrine. Continue in them, for in doing this you will save both yourself and those who hear you."

As in other passages we must ask ourselves, what kind of salvation is referred to? From what shall we be saved when we "take heed to ourselves and to the doctrine"?

First of all, without leaving the verse, it is apparent that the salvation referred to here is not the salvation of Timothy's soul. I say that because the promise is "you will save both yourself and those who hear you." Nowhere in all of Scripture does God guarantee to take someone to Heaven because of another person's faithfulness. If faithfulness were required for entrance into Heaven (which it is not), then we would each get there upon our own faithfulness. I couldn't qualify for Heaven because of your faithfulness, and you wouldn't be admitted because of my faithfulness.

So let's come back to our original question—what kind of salvation is referred to, and from what does God promise to save him? Staying in context, we read in verses 1 and 2, "Now the Spirit expressly says that in latter times some will depart from the faith, giving heed to deceiving spirits and doctrines of demons, speaking lies in hypocrisy, having their own conscience seared with a hot iron." These same false teachers are also referred to indirectly in verse 7 where

God tells Timothy to "reject profane and old wives' fables, and exercise yourself toward godliness." Then, in verse 6, God gives the promise, "If you instruct the brethren in these things, you will be a good minister of Jesus Christ, nourished in the words of faith and of the good doctrine which you have carefully followed." Notice God declares that Timothy would be a good minister of Jesus Christ if he told the brethren "these things." What things?—the warnings regarding the false teachers.

Later, in verse 15, God says, "Meditate on these things; give yourself entirely to them, that your progress may be evident to all." Please notice again that our profiting will appear to all as we meditate upon "these things." What things? The same things he's been talking about in the whole chapter—that in the light of false teachers and false teachings, Christ's ministers should be faithful. When His ministers are faithful they become "good ministers" (verse 6), the brethren are "nourished in the words of faith and of the good doctrine" (verse 6), the minister's progress becomes evident to all (verse 15), he saves himself from these "deceiving spirits and doctrines of demons" (verses 1 and 16), and he will also save or deliver those that hear him. How will he save or deliver them?—by the sound doctrine that he proclaims. That's why Paul said in verse 13, "Till I come, give attention to reading, to exhortation, to doctrine."

No, 1 Timothy 4:16 is not referring to saving our souls by

good works; it is referring, quite clearly, to saving ourselves and others under our influence from false teaching, by taking heed to ourselves and the doctrine we proclaim.

2 Timothy 4:7–8

"I have fought the good fight, I have finished the race, I have kept the faith. Finally, there is laid up for me the crown of righteousness, which the Lord, the righteous Judge, will give to me on that Day, and not to me only but also to all who have loved His appearing."

Keep in mind that salvation is always referred to in Scripture as a gift. For instance, in Romans 5, salvation is referred to as "the free gift" (verse 15), "the gift by the grace of the one Man, Jesus Christ" (verse 15), "the gift" and "the free gift" (verse 16), "the gift of righteousness" (verse 17), and "the free gift" (verse 18). Then there is the statement in Romans 6:23 that "the gift of God is eternal life through Jesus Christ our Lord." So, we see that righteousness or salvation is God's free gift which comes to man by grace when he believes in Christ (see Ephesians 2:8–9).

Therefore, when Paul speaks in 2 Timothy 4:7 of fighting the good fight, finishing his course, and keeping the faith, he obviously is not talking about receiving a free gift. The very next verse (verse 8) shows clearly that he's talking about "a crown." This crown is one he has earned, and according to

Scripture salvation or eternal life is never earned. So, this "crown of righteousness" is not at all the same as the "gift of righteousness" mentioned in Romans 5. The crown of righteousness in 2 Timothy 4 is for faithful service; the gift of righteousness in Romans 5 is a gift, received solely by faith in Christ alone. It is a gift that we receive now, without works of any kind.

Notice this very clear statement regarding this matter: "But to him who does not work but believes on Him who justifies the ungodly, his faith is accounted for righteousness" (Romans 4:5). If I receive the righteousness of God now through faith alone—apart from works of any kind—that guarantees my salvation. Having received that gift of salvation, I can then labor for my Lord to obtain rewards or crowns for faithful service. This "crown of righteousness" in 2 Timothy 4:8 is possibly synonymous with the "incorruptible crown" mentioned in 1 Corinthians 9:25— the crown also received by running the race, or being faithful. However, remember that any crowns for which we labor are earned only after we've received salvation by faith, and then from the position of already being a child of God— not in the hope of becoming His child, or remaining His child.

Crowns are one thing—given for faithful service; salvation or eternal life is quite something else—given as a free gift, apart from our works before or after we receive it, and cannot be lost.

Titus 1:1–2

"Paul, a bondservant of God and an apostle of Jesus Christ, according to the faith of God's elect and the acknowledgment of the truth which accords with godliness, in hope of eternal life which God, who cannot lie, promised before time began."

The key word in this passage in the minds of many people is the word, "hope." So often a person will read this and say something like, "You see, even the apostle Paul only hoped that he had eternal life—he didn't know that he was saved." Such a conclusion is based upon our modern use of the English word "hope." For instance, when a husband comes home from work and tells his wife that his employer is considering giving him a promotion, his wife asks, "Do you think you will get it?" And the husband replies, "I hope so." In other words, he means maybe I will and maybe I won't.

The word translated "hope" in Titus 1:2 does not mean maybe something will happen or maybe it won't happen. The closest English word we have to the Greek word translated "hope" in this verse would probably be "anticipation"—in fact, the translation would be even stronger—a joyful anticipation. In other words, a real assurance—not a nagging doubt. So, what Paul is saying in Titus is simply that God, who cannot lie, has promised eternal life to those who have faith in Christ. Paul is telling his readers that he joyfully anticipates this promise of God.

Following one of the rules of Bible interpretation listed in Appendix A, we compare other statements of Paul regarding salvation, particularly his own salvation. The following passages demonstrate Paul's assurance of salvation rather than a merely "hope-so" salvation.

> For I am not ashamed of the gospel of Christ, for it is the power of God to salvation for everyone who believes, for the Jew first and also for the Greek.
>
> Romans 1:16

The Gospel is what saves people. Who does it save? "Everyone who believes." Did Paul believe? Of course, he did. Is belief in Christ all that's required for salvation? We have already seen the abundant testimony of Scripture that salvation is given to those who believe in Christ—plus nothing else.

> For since, in the wisdom of God, the world through wisdom did not know God, it pleased God through the foolishness of the message preached to save those who believe.
>
> 1 Corinthians 1:21

How does God save according to this verse? "Through the foolishness of the message preached." Whom does he save? "Those who believe"—including the apostle Paul.

Who shall bring a charge against God's elect? It is God who justifies.
Who is he who condemns? It is Christ who died, and furthermore
is also risen, who is even at the right hand of God, who also makes
intercession for us. Who shall separate us from the love of Christ?
Shall tribulation, or distress, or persecution, or famine, or nakedness,
or peril, or sword? As it is written: "For Your sake we are killed all
day long; we are accounted as sheep for the slaughter." Yet in all
these things we are more than conquerors through Him who loved
us. For I am persuaded that neither death nor life, nor angels nor
principalities nor powers, nor things present nor things to come,
nor height nor depth, nor any other created thing, shall be able to
separate us from the love of God which is in Christ Jesus our Lord.

Romans 8:33–39

The questions asked in verses 33 and 34 with their
corresponding answers may be more accurately translated in
the following way: "Who shall bring a charge against God's
elect? Will God who justifies? Who is he that condemns?
Is it Christ who died, and furthermore is also risen?" It
is unthinkable in Paul's mind that God would charge his
children with their sin after He has given His own Son to
pay the complete penalty for that sin (verse 32). It is just
as unthinkable that the Lord Jesus Christ—the One who
actually "bore our sins in His own body on the tree"—would
condemn those He has redeemed.

Well, if God doesn't condemn believers, who or what
can? Paul replies to this question in verses 38 and 39. Satan
cannot separate us from the love of God since verse 38 says

that "angels" cannot do it. The sins that we committed today—or even those we might commit in the future—cannot condemn us because verse 38 also says that neither "things present, nor things to come" can do it. I cannot separate myself from the Lord once I know Him because verse 39 tells me that there is no "created thing" that can do it. I may not be much, but at least I could be included in the words "created thing." Neither can I be separated from the Lord by time or space, for the beginning of verse 39 says that neither "height nor depth" can separate us from the love of God which is in Christ Jesus our Lord." And remember it is the apostle Paul who is saying in verse 38, "I am persuaded" that none of these things can separate me from the Lord.

> Not by works of righteousness which we have done, but according to His mercy He saved us, through the washing of regeneration and renewing of the Holy Spirit.
>
> Titus 3:5

Paul includes himself when he says "according to His mercy He saved us." Notice, that he not only includes himself in the statement but the salvation of which he speaks has already been accomplished—"He saved us." Did Paul believe he was saved? Verse 7 says, "That having been justified by His grace we should become heirs according to the hope of eternal life." Was Paul really justified? Certainly. But someone will say that the last part of verse 7 mentions that we will be heirs according to the "hope" of eternal life. Remember, however, that "hope" means anticipation, so Paul is saying that he has been justified by God's grace, and because of that fact he will be an heir according to the sure anticipation of eternal life.

Hebrews 3:6–14

"But Christ as a Son over His own house, whose house we are if we hold fast the confidence and the rejoicing of the hope firm to the end. Therefore, as the Holy Spirit says: 'Today, if you will hear His voice, do not harden your hearts as in the rebellion, in the day of trial in the wilderness, where your fathers tested Me, tried Me, and saw My works forty years. Therefore I was angry with that generation, and said, "They always go astray in their heart, and they have not known My ways." So I swore in My wrath, "They shall not enter My rest." ' Beware, brethren, lest there be in any of you an evil heart of unbelief in departing from the living God; but exhort one another daily, while it is called 'Today,' lest any of you be hardened through the deceitfulness of sin. For we have become partakers of Christ if we hold the beginning of our confidence steadfast to the end."

In the light of other Scripture, these verses are difficult to understand at first. To be honest, they cause one to really scratch his head and wonder how these verses can fit into the very clear verses that God has given on salvation.

However, in reality, these verses state clearly just what the Bible teaches from cover to cover—and what I have been stating in this book over and over again—that only the person who is trusting Jesus Christ alone is really saved at all. The person who believes that Jesus Christ is necessary, but needs our help, is not really saved at all. The person who says he is trusting Christ, but is also holding on to water baptism or church membership or enduring to the end or being faithful or tithing or prayer is not really saved at all. Hebrews 3:6 is literally saying the following: "We are the house of Christ if we trust Him to the limit—or fully." You see, the phrases "hold fast" and "to the end" have the thought of a full, complete, unlimited trust. Only the person who fully trusts Christ alone for salvation actually has that salvation, and, therefore, is the only one who is actually the house of Christ—or, as verse 14 states it, "partakers of Christ."

These to whom God is writing in Hebrews 3 are already saved according to the earlier part of the chapter. For instance, in verse 1 they are called "holy brethren, partakers of the heavenly calling." In verse 12 again, they are called "brethren." So, these are men who already know the Lord and are His "house" and are "partakers" of Him. Why are they His house? Why are they partakers of Christ? Because of the fact that they hold fast the confidence—not hold fast their salvation—firm to the end. That is to say, the trust they have in Christ is a complete trust, and they trust Him to the end (or, to the limit).

No man, according to Scripture, is really a saved man who does not trust Jesus Christ solely, and to the limit, for his salvation. I don't mean by that, that one must trust Jesus for every detail of living. I'm speaking of salvation now. If I am depending upon anything or anyone else in place of, or in addition to, Jesus Christ, then I'm not really trusting Him "to the limit." Therefore I'm not His house, nor His son, nor partaker of Him. I am—to put it bluntly—not even saved at all, even though I may know all the terminology and claim to believe the Bible from cover to cover.

Hebrews 3:12

"Beware, brethren, lest there be in any of you an evil heart of unbelief in departing from the living God."

Again, I want you to notice that the ones addressed are "brethren"—saved people. They are being warned of having an evil heart of unbelief in departing from the living God. Some have assumed this means departing from Him to the point of being lost, but the Bible has many examples of God's children who departed from the Lord and yet were still His.

The word "departing" in this verse means "to remove or

revolt." Lot was a saved man who departed from the Lord. He pitched his tent toward Sodom and eventually lived in that wicked city and became one of its leaders. In fact, he got so involved in the affairs of the sinful, wicked city of Sodom that we read in 2 Peter 2:7 that he was "oppressed by the filthy conduct of the wicked." Yet, in that very same verse God calls him "righteous Lot." And in 2 Peter 2:8 God refers to him this way: "(for that righteous man, dwelling among them, tormented his righteous soul from day to day by seeing and hearing their lawless deeds)." What lesson is there to learn from "righteous Lot" who departed from the living God? The lesson to be learned is found in 2 Peter 2:9: "Then the Lord knows how to deliver the godly out of temptations [like Lot, and other brethren who revolt against the Lord], and to reserve the unjust [that's the unbeliever] under punishment for the day of judgment." Notice, it is the unjust who are punished in the day of judgment. The godly—even though they revolt occasionally in their lives against God—are delivered out of temptation, just as God "delivered righteous Lot" (2 Peter 2:7).

So, Hebrews 3:12 is warning Christians not to become doubtful and unbelieving regarding the promises of God, and thereby find themselves revolting against Him. Instead, they are to do what verse 13 advocates: "but exhort one another daily, while it is called 'Today,' lest any of you be hardened through the deceitfulness of sin." Many believers—both outside and inside the Bible—have been hardened through the deceitfulness of sin. God says this will not happen if we exhort one another daily. Therefore, Hebrews 3:12–13 is an exhortation to watchfulness against sin, and especially the sin of not believing God regarding His gracious promises to His children.

Hebrews 6:4–6

"For it is impossible for those who were once enlightened, and have tasted the heavenly gift, and have become partakers of the Holy Spirit, and have tasted the good word of God and the powers of the age to come, if they fall away, to renew them again to repentance, since they crucify again for themselves the Son of God, and put Him to an open shame."

Those who use this passage to teach that a man once saved may later lose his salvation usually make the following conclusions from these verses.

First, the people referred to in Hebrews 6 are really saved as seen in such phrases as that they "were once enlightened, and have tasted the heavenly gift, and have become partakers of the Holy Spirit, and have tasted the good word of God and the powers of the age to come."

Second, it is possible for these saved people to lose their salvation because it says, "if they fall away."

I certainly agree that those referred to in Hebrews 6:4–6 are genuine Christians, but if verse 6 teaches that these saved people can lose their salvation, that same verse must also teach that once their salvation is lost it can never be regained. Notice carefully what these verses say: "For it is impossible...if they fall away to renew them again to repentance." What is it impossible to do? To renew those who have fallen away to repentance.

I have spoken to many people who believe they can lose their salvation. They also believe that even though they have lost their salvation, they can repent and be saved again. But if the phrase "fall away" is the same thing as "lose your salvation," then Hebrews 6:4–6 can only mean once a saved man is lost he can never be saved again.

Well, what does Hebrews 6:4–6 mean? To answer the question we need to define certain things, for instance, the phrase, "fall away." It means basically to fall to one side—not like falling off a cliff where there's no return but rather being out of step. Also needing clarification is the phrase, "to renew them again to repentance." Perhaps a more modern way of saying it might help. Williams translates it "to keep on restoring them to their first repentance." Philips renders it "to make them repent as they did at first."

The thing that is impossible for a believer who gets out of step with the Lord is to be taken back to his original repentance—the repentance that brought him into salvation at the beginning. Why would it be impossible to do this? The last part of verse 6 tells us why: Jesus Christ would have to be crucified over again. Such a possibility is unthinkable. Berkeley brings this out in his translation, "for they repeat— so far as they are concerned—the crucifying of the Son of God afresh..."

We know that the people mentioned here are not lost because of what the writer goes on to say about them:

1. They are "rejected" (disapproved).

2. They are "near to being cursed."

These believers are similar to those mentioned in 1 Corinthians 3:11-15. They were on the foundation, Jesus Christ (verse 11). They built upon that foundation, "gold, silver, precious stones, wood, hay, straw" (verse 12). All their work will be tried by fire for its quality ("what sort it is"—verse 13). If their work endures they will receive a reward (verse 14). If their work is burned up, they shall suffer loss but "he himself will be saved, yet so as through fire" (verse 15). The subject matter of 1 Corinthians 3 is rewards. We work for rewards, but salvation is received as a gift—not of works.[14]

Hebrews 6 is also talking about rewards, not salvation. The illustration given in Hebrews 6 confirms this. In verses 7 and 8 God says, "For the earth which drinks in the rain that often comes upon it, and bears herbs useful for those by whom it is cultivated, receives blessing from God; but if it bears thorns and briars, it is rejected and near to being cursed, whose end is to be burned."

Notice, the productive earth "receives blessing from God." The nonproductive earth "bears thorns and briars [and] is rejected [disapproved] and is near to being cursed whose end is to be burned." Notice, not cursed but near—like 1 Corinthians 3:15, 'he himself shall be saved; yet so as through fire.' Again, notice that these nonproductive believers themselves are not burned but their "end" is. In other words, the end of all that they produced ("thorns and briars") is burned.

Hebrews 10:26–29

"For if we sin willfully after we have received the knowledge of the truth, there no longer remains a sacrifice for sins, but a certain fearful expectation of judgment, and fiery indignation which will devour the adversaries. Anyone who has rejected Moses' law dies without mercy on the testimony of two or three witnesses. Of how much worse punishment, do you suppose, will he be thought worthy who has trampled the Son of God underfoot, counted the blood of the covenant by which he was sanctified a common

thing, and insulted the Spirit of grace?"

It is very, very important to carefully observe the pronouns in this passage. For instance, in verse 26 we have the statement, "For if we sin willfully after we have received the knowledge of the truth, there no longer remains a sacrifice for sins." Goodspeed translates that last phrase as follows: "There is no sacrifice left to be offered for our sins." And the Twentieth Century New Testament translates it this way: "There can be no further sacrifice..." Why is there no more sacrifice for sins when we sin willfully? The answer is found in the same tenth chapter of Hebrews.

Referring to the Old Testament blood sacrifices, the writer of Hebrews says in 10:1–3:

> For the law, having a shadow of the good things to come, and not the very image of the things, can never with these same sacrifices, which they offer continually year by year, make those who approach perfect. For then would they not have ceased to be offered? For the worshipers, once purified, would have had no more consciousness of sins. But in those sacrifices there is a reminder of sins every year.

If the believers in the Old Testament had been purged or cleansed once, they would never again need another sacrifice. The problem was that the sacrifices of the Old Testament did not cleanse them. They simply covered their sins temporarily. But Christ's once-for-all sacrifice is not that way:

> By that will [by God's will] we have been sanctified through the
> offering of the body of Jesus Christ once for all. For by one offering
> He has perfected forever those who are being sanctified.
>
> Hebrews 10:10, 10:14

Then the writer adds this very pointed conclusion

> Their sins and their lawless deeds I will remember no more. Now
> where there is remission of these, there is no longer an offering for
> sin.
>
> Hebrews 10:17–18

So, when we come to verse 26, where the writer begins to
talk about the willful sins of believers, we find that when
we sin willfully after we know the Lord there are no more
sacrifices to be offered. Why? Because Christ's one sacrifice
is all sufficient for all of our sins, once and for all.

Well, if I don't have to worry about any more offering
for sins, what is left? What about God's judgment and
wrath? Where does it fall? Verse 27 begins the answer:
"But a certain fearful expectation of judgment, and fiery
indignation which will devour the adversaries." No matter
how you look at it, the believer in Christ is not an "adversary
of Christ." This word "adversary" literally means "an enemy,
an opponent, one who is in opposition to God." These
phrases do not define or describe the child of God. This
is where it becomes important to observe the pronouns.

Beginning in verse 28 we read, "Anyone who has rejected Moses' law dies without mercy on the testimony of two or three witnesses." Please take note of the change of the pronouns coming up in verse 29:

> Of how much worse punishment, do you suppose, will he be thought worthy who has trampled the Son of God underfoot, counted the blood of the covenant by which he was sanctified a common thing, and insulted the Spirit of grace? For we know Him who said, "Vengeance is Mine, I will repay," says the Lord.

Please notice that the one who will undergo "much worse punishment" is not "you," but "he." This "he" is the adversary of verse 27. And verse 29 describes three things that he (the adversary) is guilty of.

First, the adversary is guilty of rejecting Christ—"who has trampled the Son of God underfoot;" second, the adversary considers the blood of no value—"counted the blood of the covenant by which he was sanctified a common thing;" third, the adversary abuses the work of the Holy Spirit—"and insulted the Spirit of grace."

None of these things are true of Christians. A Christian, instead of rejecting Christ, trusts Him; instead of considering the blood of no value, the believer counts upon the blood to cleanse him; instead of abusing the work of the Holy Spirit, the believer has responded to the convicting work of the Spirit and has trusted Christ.

There are some, however, who point to the middle part of verse 29 and say, "Well, this man—this adversary—at one time was saved because verse 29 says, "he was sanctified." No, my dear friend, verse 29 does not say the adversary was ever sanctified. Verse 29 says the Son of God was sanctified. See it for yourself. All you have to do is ask the question, "Who was sanctified by the blood of the covenant?" The Son of God was. This adversary "has trampled the Son of God underfoot, counted the blood of the covenant by which He was sanctified a common thing."

You say, "Wait a minute! The Son of God didn't need to be sanctified. He was already holy." But the Lord Jesus Christ was sanctified. In fact, He sanctified Himself, and said so in no uncertain terms. You find it recorded in John 17:19: "And for their sakes I sanctify Myself, that they also may be sanctified by the truth."

The adversary counts the blood by which Christ was sanctified an unholy offering. There is nothing in store for such a man but the wrath and judgment of a holy God. But, thank the Lord, for those who believe in Christ there is no more sacrifice—no more offering is made for our sin— because, as God promised:

> Their sins and their lawless deeds I will remember no more. Now where there is remission of these, there is no longer an offering for sin.

> Hebrews 10:17–18

What a blessing to know that even when we sin willfully after we know the Lord, it is still that one sacrifice made by Christ on Calvary that is completely sufficient and adequate for our salvation. The poor adversary of the Lord has to look forward to judgment, but we can look forward to having all of our sins paid for, forgiven, and put behind His back, on the basis of that one wonderful sacrifice made by the Lord Jesus Christ on our behalf.

Hebrews 10:38–39

"Now the just shall live by faith; But if anyone draws back, My soul has no pleasure in him. But we are not of those who draw back to perdition, but of those who believe to the saving of the soul."

I don't know why men quote this passage to try to prove that a saved man can lose his salvation if he fails to work. Twice in the passage the value of faith is brought out. In verse 38 he says clearly that "the just shall live by faith." In verse 39, contrasting the believer with the unbeliever, he says that "we are not of those [unbelievers] who draw back to perdition; but of those who believe to the saving of the soul." Notice it does not say, "We are of them who believe, and work, and strive, and endure to the saving of the soul." It says, "we are they that believe [nothing else] to the saving of the soul." So, then, salvation in this case—as everywhere else in the Bible—hinges upon the one condition of faith in Christ.

Sometimes verse 38 is quoted to show that God says that He (God) will have no pleasure in those who draw back. I've had men—perhaps sincere—say to me something like the following: "Look! God says if you draw back He will have no pleasure in you! He doesn't say He'll have some pleasure in you." The point that such people are trying to make is that if God has "no" pleasure in someone, then that someone no longer belongs to Him. The only problem with that logic is the one speaking in verse 38 is not God, but the writer of Hebrews (the human author). "My soul" does not refer to God but the human writer. How do I know that? I know it because of the passage. Notice verses 34 and 38:

> For you had compassion on me in my chains, and joyfully accepted the plundering of your goods, knowing that you have a better and an enduring possession for yourselves in heaven.
>
> Hebrews 10:34

> Now the just shall live by faith; But if anyone draws back, my soul [the one who was in chains in verse 34] has no pleasure in him.
>
> Hebrews 10:38

No, it is not God who is saying He has no pleasure in the one who draws back. It is the writer of the epistle to the Hebrews saying it. Not only that, but in verse 34 he tells them that they already have "a better and an enduring possession for yourselves in heaven." These are the same people who "believe to the saving of the soul" (verse 39).

James 2:17

"Thus also faith by itself, if it does not have works, is dead."

The subject matter of James 2:14–26 is "what good does it do to tell another man 'I have faith' if I don't show it by my works?" James 2:14–26 has nothing to do with salvation before God; it does not involve how to receive eternal life; it does talk about the profit there is before men of demonstrating our faith. Before we observe this in James 2, I think it's important to see clearly from God's Word what He himself has to say about being justified in His eyes. James uses Abraham as an illustration of someone being justified by faith and works. However, he uses Abraham to illustrate how he was justified by faith and works before other men— as we shall soon see.

In Romans 4, God uses Abraham again as an illustration, but this time of how a man is justified by faith alone before God. In clear, unmistakable language God declares:

> What then shall we say that Abraham our father has found according to the flesh? For if Abraham was justified by works, he has something to boast about, but not before God. For what does the Scripture say? "Abraham believed God, and it was accounted to

> him for righteousness." Now to him who works, the wages are not counted as grace but as debt. But to him who does not work but believes on Him who justifies the ungodly, his faith is accounted for righteousness.
>
> Romans 4:1–5

Please notice, Abraham could be justified by works "but not before God." If a person insists that James 2 teaches a man is justified by works before God, then we have a very clear contradiction. If, on the other hand, Romans 4 is speaking of our justification before God (which it obviously is), and if James is speaking of our justification before men (which is just as obvious by a careful reading of the chapter), then we have no contradiction whatever.

Let's go back to James 2. The whole point of the passage is found in verses 14–16.

> What does it profit, my brethren, if someone says he has faith but does not have works? Can faith save him? If a brother or sister is naked and destitute of daily food, and one of you says to them, "Depart in peace, be warmed and filled," but you do not give them the things which are needed for the body, what does it profit?

Please notice, in verse 14, James is writing to "my brethren," and in verse 15 the illustration he gives is "if a brother or sister" comes to you in need. So, he's talking about believers in Christ coming to another believer in Christ in time of need. His whole point is that if the brother who could help the destitute children of God does not help those needy persons, then what profit is there? The conclusion is verse 17: "Thus also [in the same way] faith by itself, if it does not have works, is dead." Some have assumed that if faith is "dead" then it isn't there. However in this instance, the word dead means barren or unproductive. Even if you don't know any Greek, the gist of the passage makes that clear. There's no profit in a dead faith so far as your fellow Christian is concerned. "Dead" in James is like a dead battery in a car. The battery is there but it's useless in producing any power. The same is true of dead faith. It is of no value—of "no profit"—if it doesn't produce works.

Let's consider the remaining portion of the passage verse-by-verse.

Verse 18

Notice, it's a man that says, "You have faith, and I have works. Show me your faith [not, "show God your faith"] without your works, and I will show you my faith [not, "I will show God my faith"] by my works." The only way I can show you my faith is by my works. The only way you can show me your faith is by your works. But I don't have to show God my faith; He sees the heart. And, according to Romans 4, when I trust Him He counts my faith as righteousness.

Verse 19

The person who believes in one God is no better than the demons, because they not only believe that, they tremble at the thought of it. No one is ever saved just by believing in one God. Jesus said, "I am the way, the truth and the life. No man comes to the Father except through Me" (John 14:6).

Verse 20

This verse simply verifies the conclusions of earlier verses like 14, 16 and 17: that if works do not spring from faith, then that faith is nonproductive.

Verses 21–23

Abraham is a perfect example of faith cooperating with his works before men to produce a mature faith. Notice when Abraham was justified by works (verse 21). He was justified by works "when he offered Isaac his son on the altar." According to Scripture, Abraham was justified by faith alone—before God—in Genesis 15:6. At that time Isaac wasn't even born. Then, after Isaac was born and began to grow as a young man, Abraham displayed his faith in the Lord by being willing to offer his only son upon the altar. This is recorded in Genesis 22. But keep in mind, Genesis 15:6 says, "And he [Abraham] believed in the Lord, and He accounted it to him for righteousness." Abraham was justified before God by faith alone approximately fifteen years before the events in Genesis 22 took place.

James 2:22 makes it clear before whom Abraham was justified by works: "Do you see that faith was working together with his works, and by works faith was made perfect [mature or complete]?" In other words, this is the way you and I see it. We see Abraham's works, and because we see how much he was willing to trust the Lord, we know he really did have faith. James 2:23 says: "And the Scripture was fulfilled which says, 'Abraham believed God, and it was accounted to him for righteousness.' And he was called the friend of God." There are two Scriptures fulfilled in verse 23: Genesis 15:6 which says Abraham was justified by faith before God and 2 Chronicles 20:7 which says Abraham is God's friend because of his obedience. It's impossible to display faith without obedience.

Someone may say, "Well, when Abraham offered up Isaac there were no other men around to see him do it. So how could he be displaying his faith before men?" The truth of the matter is that there were other men around to see him offer up Isaac. If you will read Genesis 22:1–14, you will notice that when Abraham took Isaac to Mount Moriah he also took with him two of his young men (verse 3). Abraham, an old man by this time, "saw the place afar off" (verse 4). He turned to his young men and told them to stay with the donkey, while he and Isaac went to the place to which he pointed, to offer a burnt offering (verse 5). If

Abraham could see the place, then there's no doubt the young men could certainly see it and did see it. The obvious observer, of course, was Isaac. He certainly had a front row seat!

James 2 sums up with the phrase in verse 24, "You see then that a man is justified by works, and not by faith only." Notice it carefully: You see it this way—not God. Before God we are justified by faith alone; before men, by faith and works. God sees the heart and our faith. Man does not see the heart; therefore, he must see works. And when he sees works (verses 18, 22, 24), then he knows that the person displaying those works has faith.

There is no hint in this entire passage of a believer losing salvation because he doesn't work. Instead, it is an exhortation to join works with our faith to have profit and to be productive and fruitful for the Lord, especially among our fellow "brothers and sisters" (verses 14–15).

2 Peter 2:20–22

For if, after they have escaped the pollutions of the world through the knowledge of the Lord and Savior Jesus Christ, they are again entangled in them and overcome, the latter end is worse for them than the beginning. For it would have been better for them not to have known the way of righteousness, than having known it, to turn from the holy commandment delivered to them. But it has happened to them according to the true proverb: "A dog returns to his own vomit," and, "a sow, having washed, to her wallowing in the mire."

It is sometimes taught from this passage that those referred to in these verses are former Christians who have become apostates. They once believed in Christ (verse 20), but later turned from the holy commandment (verse 21), and now their latter end is worse than the beginning (verse 20). They have returned to their sin and their ungodly ways.

The only thing I can say to this interpretation is that it does not do justice to the passage or to the Scripture as a whole. To know of whom Peter is speaking in these verses we must identify who "they" refers to in verse 20. "For if after they have escaped the pollutions of the world...the latter end is worse for them...for it would have been better for them...than, having known it...the holy commandment delivered to them...but it has happened to them according to the true proverb." Who is this passage referring to? If we simply remember to stay in context we can find out quite easily. In verses 1 and 2, Peter tells us of whom he is writing. "But there were also false prophets among the people, even as there will be false teachers among you, who will secretly bring in destructive heresies, even denying the Lord who bought them, and bring on themselves swift destruction. And many will follow their destructive ways, because of whom the way of truth will be blasphemed." Therefore, the "they" and the "them" of 2 Peter 2:20–22 refer to "false teachers" (verse 1). The subject is not true teachers who have turned sour, but false teachers who shall come in secretly among "you" (the believer, verse 1).

The identification of these people as false teachers is further borne out in the following verses.

Verse 3

"By covetousness they will exploit you with deceptive words; for a long time their judgment has not been idle, and their destruction does not slumber."

Notice, it does not say "your" destruction does not slumber. It says "their" destruction does not slumber.

Verse 9

"The Lord knows how to deliver the godly [the saved] out of temptations, and to reserve the unjust [the unsaved—in this case, the false teacher] under punishment for the day of judgment."

Verse 10

"And especially those who walk according to the flesh in the lust of uncleanness and despise authority. They are presumptuous, self-willed." Again, notice that it does not say, "Presumptuous are you."

Verse 12
"But these, like natural brute beasts made to be caught and destroyed, speak evil of the things they do not understand, and will utterly perish in their own corruption."

Verse 17
"These are wells without water, clouds carried by a tempest, for whom is reserved the blackness of darkness forever."

Verse 18
"For when they speak great swelling words of emptiness, they allure through the lusts of the flesh."

Not only is it true that those referred to here are false prophets because of the context, but also because of what they are called. In verse 22 God says, "But it has happened to them according to the true proverb: 'A dog returns to his own vomit,' and, 'a sow, having washed, to her wallowing in the mire.'" Nowhere in this verse—or in the entire passage— are these men referred to as "sheep," but all the way through God's Word true believers are called Christ's sheep. They are never called dogs and never called pigs. Those who belong to Jesus Christ are sheep, and are called such over and over again throughout Scripture. Notice the following examples.

I am the door of the sheep.

John 10:7

I am the good shepherd. The good shepherd gives His life for the sheep.

John 10:11

I am the good shepherd, and I know my sheep, and am known by My own.

John 10:14

But you do not believe, because you are not of My sheep, as I said to you. My sheep hear my voice, and I know them, and they follow Me. And I give them eternal life, and they shall never perish; neither shall anyone snatch them out of my hand.

John 10:26–28

He said to him the third time, 'Simon, son of Jonah, do you love Me?' Peter was grieved because He said to him the third time, 'Do you love Me?' And he said to Him, 'Lord, You know all things; You know that I love You.' Jesus said to him, 'Feed My sheep.

John 21:17

The Lord is my shepherd; I shall not want. He makes me to lie down in green pastures; He leads me beside the still waters

Psalm 23:1–2

Know that the Lord, He is God; It is He who has made us, and not we ourselves; we are His people and the sheep of His pasture.

Psalm 100:3

Shepherd the flock of God which is among you, serving as overseers, not by compulsion but willingly, not for dishonest gain but eagerly; nor as being lords over those entrusted to you, but being examples to the flock; and when the Chief Shepherd appears, you will receive the crown of glory that does not fade away.

1 Peter 5:2–4

Now may the God of peace who brought up our Lord Jesus from the dead, that great Shepherd of the sheep, through the blood of the everlasting covenant.

Hebrews 13:20

On the other hand, the unbeliever—though he may pretend to be one of Christ's sheep—is often called a dog or something worse. Consider these clear statements of Scripture:

Beware of false prophets, who come to you in sheep's clothing, but inwardly they are ravenous wolves.

Matthew 7:15

Notice that these false prophets put on clothes resembling sheep. But "inwardly" they are really wolves. They are not sheep who have become wolves. They are wolves pretending to be sheep. This is where so much confusion arises. We can all point to people that we've known who said they were Christians and yet who later denied the faith. Sometimes—foolishly, I'm afraid—a few will say that these were Christians who lost their salvation. In reality, however, according to Scripture, they were wolves dressed up like sheep, and no doubt even imitating the sheep's baaaa!

> Finally, my brethren, rejoice in the Lord. For me to write the same things to you is not tedious, but for you it is safe. Beware of dogs, beware of evil workers, beware of the mutilation!
>
> Philippians 3:1–2

It's interesting to note that the "brethren" are warned against the "dogs." Verse 2 does not say, "beware of becoming dogs." Instead, it tells the brethren to "beware of dogs." So then, the brethren are not the dogs, and the dogs are not the brethren!

> But outside are dogs and sorcerers and sexually immoral and murderers and idolaters, and whoever loves and practices a lie.
>
> Revelation 22:15

This passage is describing the New Jerusalem (21:1–2). Outside of the New Jerusalem are the dogs; inside are the sheep.

One phrase in 2 Peter 2:20 that has puzzled many is that these false prophets are said to have "escaped the pollutions of the world through the knowledge of the Lord and Savior Jesus Christ." So, the reasoning goes, if they've known the Lord Jesus Christ, then they were saved at one time. The problem is immediately cleared up when we understand the meaning of the word "knowledge." It is true that anyone who knows Christ is saved. In fact, Jesus himself said, "And this is eternal life, that they may know You, the only true God, and Jesus Christ whom You have sent" (John 17:3). The word "know" in this verse in John is the Greek word "ginosko," and it means a personal, firsthand knowledge of a thing or person. The word translated "knowledge" in 2 Peter 2:20 is the Greek word "epignosis," and it means a recognition or an acknowledgment—not a personal, experiential knowledge.

Let me illustrate what I mean. I know my wife, Kathy. I am personally acquainted with her. I know her experientially. We are members of the same family. In John 17:3 this is the meaning of the word "know" which comes from the Greek word meaning to know personally.

I know about Martin Luther King, Winston Churchill, and the President of the United States, but I do not personally know any of these three. I acknowledge them, I recognize their photographs when I see them, I know some things about them, but I do not personally know them. In 2 Peter 2:20 this is the meaning of the word translated "knowledge" which comes from the Greek word meaning to recognize or acknowledge.

So, it is plain to see that these false teachers (2 Peter 2:1) acknowledged Christ, recognized who He was, but never knew Him personally. In light of all the knowledge they had about Him their "latter end is worse with them than the beginning." Why? Because the more light a person has the more severely he'll be punished by a holy God if he refuses to respond to that light (see Matthew 11:20–24). Second Peter 2 (the entire chapter) paints a horrible picture of the man who dares to pretend to be a Christian while in reality he is not, and is actually preaching against Christ. The things describing such a false teacher could never be attributed to a true child of God.

1 John 2:5

"But whoever keeps His word, truly the love of God is perfected in him. By this we know that we are in Him."

The epistle of 1 John is a great assurance book. The key word of the book is the word "know." In this epistle God gives the believer various ways that he may know that he really does belong to the Lord or is walking in fellowship. The really conclusive and objective means of assurance is God's own spoken word as in 1 John 5:9–13, especially verse 13: "These things I have written to you who believe in the name of the Son of God, that you may know that you have eternal life, and that you may continue to believe in the name of the Son of God."

However, there are also experiential ways for the

believer to know that he is right with the Lord in his walk. A number of these are listed in 1 John. For instance, in 2:5 we are told that we can know we are in Him when we see ourselves keeping His Word. That doesn't mean that we must keep His Word in order to know Him. It means that if we find ourselves keeping His Word, and having His love perfected in us, that's evidence to us that we know Him or are "abiding" in Him, speaking of our walk. Therefore, it gives us added assurance.

The same type of thing is mentioned in 3:14 where God says, "We know that we have passed from death to life, because we love the brethren. He who does not love his brother abides in death." In my young Christian life this was a great proof to me that I must be a child of God—and something real and genuine had actually happened in my life. You see, before I knew the Lord I wasn't really very fond of people at all. Having been born with a double harelip and cleft palate, and having gone through much ridicule from other people, I had no great affection for anyone. But a strange thing happened after I trusted Christ. I found myself beginning to love people. As a matter of fact, I discovered that I stopped thinking of people in terms of their color, or their nationality, or their economic standing. Instead, I was amazed to find that I had—although I didn't understand from where—a real genuine love for people of all sorts. This was evidence to me that something actually had happened when I trusted Christ, and this is one of the things John is talking about in his epistle.

What John is not saying in his epistle is, "This is how to tell if another person is saved;" or "This is how to be saved—love the brethren, keep His Word, or keep His commandments." No, he is not telling us to be saved by doing these things; nor is he telling us to be "fruit inspectors" of other people's lives. He is giving us guidelines and personal assurances that if we see some of these things in our lives, these are further evidences that we actually belong to the Lord.

However, the real evidence is God's promise. He promised in 5:10–12 the following:

> He who believes in the Son of God has the witness in himself; he who does not believe God has made Him a liar, because he has not believed the testimony that God has given of His Son. And this is the testimony: that God has given us eternal life, and this life is in His Son. He who has the Son has life; he who does not have the Son of God does not have life.

Based upon this passage and verse 13, if we believe the testimony God gave of His Son then we have eternal life, because this life is in His Son. That is our unshakable assurance. God said it. That settles it forever and ever. These other things mentioned in 1 John are just simply other ways we may also tell if we have experienced the miracle of the new birth through faith in Christ, or that we are abiding in Christ in our personal relationship with Him. There is no hint in any of these verses that we will lose our salvation if these qualities are lacking in our lives.

Revelation 2:7

"To him who overcomes I will give to eat from the tree of life, which is in the midst of the Paradise of God."

As is so often done, one word is interpreted in such a way as to infer that a person must do more than believe in Christ to be assured of salvation. The word in this case is "overcomes."

How often I've heard people say something like the following: "Only those who love the Lord Jesus with all their hearts and really serve Him faithfully—the overcomers—shall eat of the tree of life." Well, I have to agree that only overcomers eat of the tree of life. The important question is, who are the overcomers and how do they overcome? We answer Scripture with Scripture, remembering to interpret the somewhat unclear by that which is crystal clear. 1 John 5:5 answers the question, "Who is an overcomer?" The answer: "Who is he who overcomes the world, but he who believes that Jesus is the Son of God." 1 John 5:4 answers the second question: "How do they overcome?" The answer: "For whatever is born of God overcomes the world. And this is the victory that has overcome the world—our faith." So the overcomers are believers. How do they overcome?—by faith.

Overcoming, then, is not—as some would have us believe — a great struggling or striving for more and more goodness, but it is simply being born into God's family. God puts it this way in John 1:12–13:

> But as many as received Him, to them He gave the right to become children of God, to those who believe in His name: who were born, not of blood, nor of the will of the flesh, nor of the will of man, but of God.

Revelation 22:14

"Blessed are those who do His commandments, that they may have the right to the tree of life, and may enter through the gates into the city."

It is said by some that eating the tree of life and entering in through the gates of the city are synonymous with being saved. Therefore, this verse is teaching that in order to be saved you must "do his commandments." Well, does eating of the tree of life and entering in through the gates of the city mean the same thing as being saved? Let's find out from Scripture.

In Revelation 20:15 the Bible says: And anyone not found written in the Book of Life was cast into the lake of fire. Then, if you ignore the chapter divisions, it goes right on to say:

> Now I saw a new heaven and a new earth, for the first heaven and the first earth had passed away. Also there was no more sea. Then I, John, saw the holy city, New Jerusalem, coming down out of heaven from God, prepared as a bride adorned for her husband.

The Lord, through the apostle John, then continues to describe that city. The city is not Heaven, but the city comes down from God out of Heaven.

Before this city comes down out of Heaven and before this new Heaven and new earth is created, all the unsaved dead are brought before God, judged, and sent to the Lake of Fire (Revelation 20:11–15). So, when the new Heaven, the new earth, and the new Jerusalem are created, all the unbelievers are already confined to hell. There are no unbelievers in the new Heaven or the new earth or the new Jerusalem. Chapters 21 and 22 describe this New Jerusalem. Chapter 21 even gives the measurements of the city. Then in 22:1–2 we have a description of the water of life and the tree of life which are located in the city.

> And he showed me a pure river of water of life, clear as crystal, proceeding from the throne of God and of the Lamb. In the middle of its street, and on either side of the river, was the tree of life, which bore twelve fruits, each tree yielding its fruit every month. The leaves of the tree were for the healing of the nations.

The water of life proceeds out of God's throne. The tree of life, which is apparently not just one tree because it grows in the midst of the street and on both sides of the river, will bear 12 different kinds of fruit, a different fruit every month. And the leaves of that tree will heal the nations.

When we come to verse 14 of Chapter 22, we are told that those who do the Lord's commandments—in other words, those who obey Him—may do two things. They may eat of the tree of life and they may enter in through the gates of the New Jerusalem. These obviously are two great privileges that the obedient believer shall have. But remember, the tree of life is in the city and the city comes down from Heaven. The city is not Heaven; it is only a part of Heaven. Christ said, "In My Father's house are many mansions; if it were not so, I would have told you. I go to prepare a place for you" (John 14:2). The New Jerusalem is obviously the most glorious mansion of Heaven, but it is not the only one. And those who know the Lord and are obedient to Him will have the right to enter in through the gates of the New Jerusalem and also to eat the 12 manner of fruit of the tree of life. We cannot say for certain what that entails, but it is obviously a great privilege.

But as we have said before regarding other passages, we must also say regarding this verse, that there is no hint in Revelation 22:14 that one who does not "do His commandments" will lose his salvation. That is not even the subject matter. It is not even hinted in this verse. On the contrary, this is a picture of faithful servants being rewarded with high and very great privileges.

Important Questions to Consider

As there were important passages to consider to clear the air to the true believer's security in Christ, so there are related questions that need clarification. Here are four questions that seem to consistently pop up when the assurance of salvation is discussed.

Is Judas Iscariot a Good Example of a Saved Man Who Became Lost?

Those who believe Judas was a saved man who became lost, reason that since Judas was a disciple of the Lord, he was saved. When Jesus prayed for the disciples He said, "none of them is lost except the son of perdition"—referring to Judas (John 17:12). So it is often assumed that Judas lost his salvation when Satan "entered him" (Luke 22:3; John 13:2) and he then betrayed Christ while in his lost condition.

There are at least two flaws in this line of reasoning. The first one is the assumption that all who are disciples of the Lord are saved. By disciple, people usually mean one who is serving the Lord. But the word disciple simply means "learner." Ideally, disciples should be saved before they start learning, but unfortunately many people are busy "learning to serve the Lord" who never have been saved. Christ spoke of such disciples in Matthew 7:22–23. These "disciples" will one day stand before Christ and cry, "Lord, Lord, have we not prophesied in Your name, cast out demons in Your name, and done many wonders in Your name?" (verse 22). In other words, they were serving the Lord. Notice, they did all of these things in the name of Christ. What will be the reaction of the Lord to these people? He tells us in very clear terms: "I never knew you; depart from Me, you who practice lawlessness!" (verse 23). It is so important to realize that Jesus did not say, "Depart from me, you whom I once knew." He never knew them. Were they disciples or learners? Certainly. Were they saved and later on lost? Not at all. They were never saved to begin with. The same was true of Judas.

This brings us to the second flaw in this reasoning: that Judas became lost when Satan entered him and he then betrayed Christ. However, he was Satan's instrument before he betrayed Christ. In John 6:70-71, John recounts a coversation Jesus had with his disciples long before Satan entered Judas: "Jesus answered them, 'Did I not choose you, the twelve, and one of you is a devil?' He spoke of Judas Iscariot." So we see that even then—before the last supper, before the betrayal, before Satan entered Judas—he was already a devil or demon! For Christ to have described him this way, he could not possibly have been saved.

Can a Saved Person "Fall From Grace?"

According to the Word of God there is only one type of person who can fall from grace—the unbeliever who is attempting to work his way to Heaven. I realize that many people think that the Christian can "fall from grace." Actually it is the counterfeit Christian, the make-believe Christian, that falls from grace. It is the man who uses all the Christian terms and even lives the so-called Christian life and is depending upon that for his salvation who has fallen from grace, and is, therefore, not even saved.

God describes the person who falls from grace in the following passages:

> Indeed I, Paul, say to you that if you become circumcised, Christ will profit you nothing.
>
> Galatians 5:2

> You have become estranged from Christ, you who attempt to be justified by law; you have fallen from grace.
>
> Galatians 5:4

According to these verses, to whom is Christ of no profit? The person who is attempting to be "justified by the law." Who is fallen from grace? This same person who is attempting to be justified before God by keeping the law.

If anything is clear in Scripture, it is clear that if a man is trying to be justified or saved by law keeping, such a man is not saved at all—he is not a Christian in the Biblical sense of the word. God declares this truth very plainly in this same book of Galatians:

> Knowing that a man is not justified by the works of the law but by faith in Jesus Christ, even we have believed in Christ Jesus, that we might be justified by faith in Christ and not by the works of the law; for by the works of the law no flesh shall be justified.
>
> Galatians 2:16

> I do not set aside the grace of God; for if righteousness comes through the law, then Christ died in vain.
>
> Galatians 2:21

> But that no one is justified by the law in the sight of God is evident, for "the just shall live by faith." Yet the law is not of faith, but "the man who does them shall live by them." Christ has redeemed us from the curse of the law, having become a curse for us.
>
> Galatians 3:11–13

So then, the person in Galatians 5:4 who is attempting to be "justified by the law" is not a Christian who has lost his salvation, but just the opposite—an unbelieving, self-righteous, law-keeping sinner who refuses to be saved by grace, even though he is part of a Christian assembly.

Another thing to think about in relation to falling from grace is that even if a believer could fall from grace, falling from grace is not the same thing as falling from salvation. We have recorded, in Titus 2:11 the following clear statement: "For the grace of God that brings salvation has appeared to all men." Notice, God's grace brings salvation—it is not the same thing as salvation. Any time a man attempts to be saved by his own works, he is trying to be saved on a level far below grace—he has fallen from (or come short of) the grace that God offers. But there is nowhere in God's Word where anyone ever falls from salvation. Only the unbeliever who is attempting to work for his salvation is able to fall from grace.

How Many of the Believers' Sins Are Paid for and Forgiven?

The thought is often expressed by those who feel they can lose their salvation that only their past sins were paid for or forgiven, while in reality Scripture teaches that all sins—for believers and unbelievers alike—have already been paid for by Christ on Calvary. In addition to that, when one believes in Christ, all of his sins are forgiven—past, present and future. This is denied by many people who do not believe that a genuine believer in Christ is eternally secure.

Sometimes the following verse is quoted in the attempt to prove that only our past sins are forgiven: "Whom God set forth as a propitiation by His blood, through faith, to demonstrate His righteousness, because in His forbearance God had passed over the sins that were previously committed" (Romans 3:25). The phrase "God passed over the sins that were previously committed" refers to sins committed in previous times before Calvary.

Conybeare translates this phrase, "God had passed over the former sins of men in the times that are gone by." Revised Standard Version says, "He had passed over former sins." NASB says, "He passed over the sins previously committed." Following this train of thought Hebrews 9:15 gives added insight: "And for this reason He is the Mediator of the new covenant, by means of death, for the redemption of the transgressions under the first covenant, that those who are called may receive the promise of the eternal inheritance." The first covenant refers to the covenant that was given in the Old Testament before the Messiah came. Sins during that time were passed over because the sacrifices were only a temporary covering for their sins, which is the meaning of atonement. When Christ died, the sin debt for all men for all times was fully paid—not just covered.

So, the thought that Paul expressed in Romans 3:25 was not that his own past sins were forgiven, but that the sins committed previously to the time of Christ's death were propitiated by His payment. You see, Christ's death took care of the believers before Calvary, as well as those who believe on Him today. Those who lived before Christ, were saved by faith in His coming redemption. Those who believe in Christ today are saved by a faith in a completed redemption that He has already made on the cross.

But what about the future sins of believers? Can they be forgiven before those sins are actually committed? It's important to realize first of all that when Jesus died on the cross all of our sins were future—none of them were past. Also to answer this question, we must realize that there are two kinds of forgiveness in Scripture. There is a once-for-all forgiveness which has in view the believer's destiny. Then there is forgiveness of the Christian as a child of God which has to do with his fellowship. The first kind of forgiveness—which makes possible our entrance into Heaven—is referred to in Colossians 2:13: "And you, being dead in your trespasses and the uncircumcision of your flesh, He has made alive together with Him, having forgiven you all trespasses." Notice, He already has made us alive, and has already forgiven us of all of our trespasses. This is further borne out in Colossians 1:13–14 where God says: "He has delivered us from the power of darkness and conveyed us into the kingdom of the Son of His love, in whom we have redemption through His blood, the forgiveness of sins."

Because we have already been forgiven of all trespasses,

God can then say in Hebrews 10:14 the following: "For by one offering He has perfected forever those who are being sanctified." The one offering was given when Christ died on Calvary. At that time God perfected forever the sanctified ones—the saints. After saying we are perfected forever in verse 14, God goes on to say in verses 17 and 18:

> Their sins and their lawless deeds I will remember no more. Now where there is remission of these, there is no longer an offering for sin.

However, there is a forgiveness that we need as children to maintain a close and sweet fellowship with our Father. This is described in 1 John, especially in Chapter One. In verses 3 and 4 the apostle John says, "that you also may have fellowship with us; and truly our fellowship is with the Father and with His Son Jesus Christ. And these things we write to you that your joy may be full." Notice he does not say, "These things we write to you that you may obtain salvation." The subject is fellowship and the joy that comes along with it. John goes on to add in verses 6–9:

> If we say that we have fellowship with Him, and walk in darkness, we lie and do not practice the truth. But if we walk in the light as He is in the light, we have fellowship with one another, and the blood of Jesus Christ His Son cleanses us from all sin. If we say that we have no sin, we deceive ourselves, and the truth is not in us. If we confess

our sins, He is faithful and just to forgive us our sins and to cleanse us
from all unrighteousness.

Yes, we need forgiveness and cleansing as children to
maintain a close fellowship with the Lord and be usable
instruments in His hands. However, that forgiveness is not
to be confused with that once-for-all forgiveness that we
receive the minute we believe in Christ.

Can a Christian's Name Be Blotted Out of the Book of Life?

It is often assumed that when a person believes in Christ
his name is placed in the Book of Life; but, if he sins later on
and loses his salvation, his name is supposedly blotted out
of that book. Such, however, is not the teaching of Scripture
concerning the Book of Life.

According to God's Word, the Book of Life (which
can also be accurately translated, "the book of the living")
contains in it the names of all living people. Those who
die in unbelief are apparently blotted out of it. Those who
believe in Christ have their names left in. Then when the
time comes at the Great White Throne Judgment for God to
cast all of the unbelievers into the Lake of Fire, He will look
into the Book of Life, and those whose names are not there
(because by that time only believers' names will remain)

will be cast into the Lake of Fire. Revelation 20:15 records it: "And anyone not found written in the Book of Life was cast into the lake of fire."

But, you ask, "Where do you get the idea that everyone's names are in the Book of Life?" I get that idea from Psalm 69:28 where the Psalmist pleads with the Lord to "Let them be blotted out of the book of the living, and not be written with the righteous." It is important to find out who the "them" is in verse 28. As you read in earlier parts of the chapter, the "them" of this verse are the unbelievers. They are called "enemies" in verse 18, "adversaries" in verse 19, and described in verse 26 as "they [who] persecute the ones You have struck." The Psalmist pleads with the Lord to:

> Let their table become a snare before them, and their well-being a trap. Let their eyes be darkened, so that they do not see; and make their loins shake continually. Pour out Your indignation upon them, and let Your wrathful anger take hold of them. Let their dwelling place be desolate; let no one live in their tents. For they persecute the ones You have struck, and talk of the grief of those You have wounded. Add iniquity to their iniquity, and let them not come into Your righteousness. Let them be blotted out of the book of the living, and not be written with the righteous.
>
> Psalm 69:22–28

So, you see, these are unbelievers whom he is asking God to blot out of the book of the living. And, of course, God will blot them out of the book of the living if they die in their unbelief. He does that to all unbelievers. And so, at the Great White Throne Judgment they are not "found" written in the Book of Life.

However, there is not a single line of Scripture that ever indicates that the believer's name is blotted out of the book of life. In fact Revelation 3:5 clearly shows just the opposite: "He who overcomes shall be clothed in white garments, and I will not blot out his name from the Book of Life; but I will confess his name before My Father and before His angels."

As previously explained in Chapter Eight, some people read this verse and immediately jump to the conclusion (because of the word "overcomes") that a believer must work really hard and strive or his name will be blotted out of the Book of Life. This is not what God is saying at all. What He is saying in simple terms is that He will not blot the name of believers out of the Book of Life. Some argue, "But it doesn't say 'he who believes,' it says, 'he who overcomes.' " Yes, I agree with that. But God's Word defines who the overcomers are in 1 John 5:4–5:

> For whatever is born of God overcomes the world. And this is the victory that has overcome the world—our faith. Who is he who overcomes the world, but he who believes that Jesus is the Son of God?

So, comparing Scripture with Scripture, we see that the overcomer is the believer, and God is promising the believer in Revelation 3:5 that He will not blot his name out of the Book of Life. This indicates that the unbeliever's name will be blotted out of the Book of Life. And, as I stated previously, when the Book of Life is opened at the Great White Throne Judgment (Revelation 20:15) only the names of believers will remain. Therefore, when the names of the unbelievers are not found in the Book of Life they will be cast into the Lake of Fire. This is a far cry from the theory that a believer's name may be blotted out of the Book of Life. Nothing of the sort is ever taught in God's Word.

The Key Issue

We've covered a lot of ground in this small volume, and hopefully we have answered some puzzling questions you may have had. At least, I hope so. But there is one thing we do not ever want to minimize or forget, and that is the clarity and simplicity of the Gospel. So as we near the end of the book I'd like to remind you of the necessity of coming back to the basic truth of God's only way of salvation.

The Bible very clearly states in Ephesians 2:8–9 that it is "by grace you have been saved through faith, and that not of yourselves; it is the gift of God, not of works, lest anyone should boast." I want you to especially notice the statement, "For by grace are you saved." In our entire discussion of salvation and the security of the believer everything boils down to this very basic issue: How is a man saved? Or, how is a man's salvation sustained and maintained? The Word of God says it is by grace.

Grace by its very definition means unmerited favor—it is mercy in its purest and highest form. If we are saved by mercy, then it is obvious we do not deserve it, we cannot merit it, earn it, purchase it, or in any way do anything that would coerce God or obligate God to save us. In other words, there is nothing in and of ourselves that could make God feel that He would have to save us because of something we are or something we have done. This is also stated in Ephesians 2:8, when it says that salvation is "not of yourselves."

Therefore, anything that is of merit (any effort, work, or striving of any kind) could not be a part of our salvation. Nor could any work or duty that we perform have any part in it because verse 9 says that salvation is "not of works."

But there are some—perhaps well-meaning people— who believe that somehow grace and works go together in salvation; that they should be mingled. It is sometimes stated this way, "Yes, the Lord Jesus Christ has done His part in dying for our sins and making it possible for us to be saved. But it doesn't stop there. We've got to do our part." By "our part" it is usually implied or meant that there is some kind of work or duty we must perform in order to get saved or to remain saved. Though it is true, according to Ephesians 2:10, that good works should follow salvation by grace; it is not true that good works and grace are equally important or necessary in salvation. Ephesians 2:10 puts it this way: "For we are His workmanship, created in Christ Jesus for good works, which God prepared beforehand that we should walk in them." In other words, it is normal for good works to follow salvation. That does not mean it is mandatory, or if they do not follow that it is proof that one

The Key Issue | 183

is not saved, as we've already seen regarding the four kinds of Christians in John 15. Remember, the first type of branch bore no fruit at all, and was therefore taken home. Such a condition, however, is subnormal. The norm is that those who are saved by grace—and grace alone—should then walk in the good works which God has planned for them.

While admitting and recognizing all of the above, we must come back again to the basic issue at hand: Is a man saved by grace, or by works, or by a combination of the two? According to Scripture (Ephesians 2:8–9; Titus 3:5; Romans 4:1–5), salvation is by grace. But not only is salvation by grace; the Bible also teaches that salvation is by grace alone. Read and carefully analyze the following verse. "And if by grace, then it is no longer of works; otherwise grace is no longer grace. But if it is of works, it is no longer grace; otherwise work is no longer work" (Romans 11:6). This whole passage is talking about God's elective principle in salvation. This principle is the grace principle, and the Lord makes it perfectly clear in this one verse that if salvation is by grace then it cannot be in any way of works. To make salvation by grace and of works robs grace of its very character. Read it again: "And if by grace, then it is no longer of works; otherwise grace is no longer grace." To illustrate, if I took one shoe and one sock off and left one of each on, you couldn't say I was barefoot; nor could you say I had my shoes and socks on. I'd be half and half. Well, in salvation there is no half and half. Salvation is either totally by grace or it is totally by works—"if it is of works, it is no longer grace; otherwise work is no longer work." Salvation is not—nor can it be—a combination of grace and works. Perhaps Romans 4:1–5 is the clearest passage to illustrate this.

God uses Abraham as an example in this passage. Abraham, you may recall, lived 430 years before the law was given. God says regarding him: "What then shall we say that Abraham our father has found according to the flesh? For if Abraham was justified by works, he has something to boast about, but not before God." God is simply saying that Abraham could have been justified by works—but never before God—only before men. Continuing in this passage, the question is asked, "For what does the Scripture say? Abraham believed God, and it was accounted to him for righteousness." Notice, that the patriarch, Abraham, had God's righteousness deposited to his account by faith—not by works. Note especially the fourth verse: "Now to him who works, the wages are not counted as grace but as debt." To put it in modern English, if you work for something, it is owed to you. If you work 40 hours on the job, your employer owes you your salary—he doesn't give it to you out of the bigness of his heart. Similarly in salvation, if you work for it in any way, then God is indebted to you—He must give you your just reward. But salvation is never called a reward in

Scripture. It is always "a gift."

But, to continue with God's illustration in Romans 4, He then goes on to say in verse 5, "But to him who does not work but believes on Him who justifies the ungodly, his faith is accounted for righteousness." So, here is the picture that we have thus far: Just like Abraham could not be justified in the eyes of God by working, so a man today cannot be justified in the eyes of God by working. In fact, as soon as anyone tries to work to gain salvation, salvation is no longer by grace; instead it would be a debt that must be paid. But, to the man who does no work but trusts in the Lord Jesus Christ (He who justifies the ungodly), that man's faith is counted for righteousness. Salvation cannot be part grace and part works.

As soon as we move to the subject of serving the Lord after we are saved, then we can talk all we want to about works. However, even then we must be careful to recognize that working for our Heavenly Father once we are saved still does not in any way bring, keep, maintain, sustain, or guarantee our salvation. Being saved is completely and only by God's grace. And when the Bible says it is by His grace, it does not mean that it is His grace that enables us to work so we can earn salvation! Keep in mind that the Biblical definition for grace includes the absence of all works. It cannot be by grace and works. Salvation is not by mercy and at the same time earned. The two are diametrically opposed to one another as far as salvation is concerned.

This, then, is the issue. It is clear that one may have good works—and be sincere in them—without believing in Christ, and that one would still be lost. It is equally clear from the Bible, although not very often in the minds of men, that one may have works and believe in Christ and still not be saved. The reason is found in the Biblical definition. To believe, Biblically speaking, means to trust or to rely upon. So if, in the Biblical sense of the word, I believe in Christ, then I am relying upon Him, solely and totally, to take me to Heaven when I die. Just as grace means that salvation is totally of God and not of anything that we do, so belief in Christ is relying totally upon the Person and the work of the Lord Jesus Christ, and not in anything of myself, my church, my minister, my priest, or my rabbi. How often men say, "Well, I believe in Christ and I'm working too, so my work won't hurt me. It can only help." The problem is such people are not really believing in Christ in the Biblical sense of the word—and the Biblical sense of the word is the only sense that is really valid. We dare not trust in a Christ of our own making; we dare not believe our own way; and we dare not define grace or belief as we want to. We must go back to the Bible. And the Bible makes clear that to believe in Christ is to trust solely and only in Him and His work for our salvation.

Therefore, if your definitions of grace and belief do

not correspond to those of the Bible, why not right now—instead of trusting anything of yourself—trust solely and wholly upon the Lord Jesus Christ. The moment you do that, Christ guarantees, "Most assuredly, I say to you, he who believes in Me has everlasting life" (John 6:47). There is no other salvation. All other so-called salvations are actually probations.

Perhaps in reading this book you have understood that you may know God personally through faith in the Lord Jesus Christ, and you have made the choice to believe in Him as your Savior. On the other hand, maybe you previously trusted in Christ to save you but have been weighed down with doubts or fears about your salvation. In either case, I want to remind you of two of God's great promises. There is that strong guarantee in 1 John 5:13: "These things I have written to you who believe in the name of the Son of God, that you may know that you have eternal life." Then in Matthew 11:28–29 Jesus invited us by saying, "Come to Me, all you who labor and are heavy laden, and I will give you rest. Take My yoke upon you and learn from Me, for I am gentle and lowly in heart, and you will find rest for your souls." We believe, we come, and He gives us eternal life and rest for our souls. He's certainly worthy of our trust.

Appendix A

Is There a Proper Way to Interpret the Bible?

There are many interpretations of the Bible, but still only one Bible. How can you know what the Bible actually means and what it teaches? How can you be assured that what I have shared with you in *The Gift of God* is accurate and true to the Scriptures? Here are some suggestions that will help you decide for yourself what is or is not a true interpretation of the Bible.

To give you an idea of how I approach the study of the Bible, I would like to explain nine solid principles of proper Bible interpretation. Faithfully follow these principles and your Bible will open up to you as never before.

- *Where the Bible speaks literally, accept its teaching literally.*

- *Consider to whom any given Scripture is addressed.*

- *Consider the contents of the verse or passage under consideration. (What's actually in the verse or verses?)*

- *Consider the context of any statement. By context I mean the verses around the particular statement. For instance, when Jesus said in John 7:38, "He who believes in Me, as the Scripture has said, out of his heart will flow rivers of living water," to what was He referring? The best way to find out is to read the verses that surround this one. In this case, the very next verse clearly says, "But this He spoke concerning the Spirit, whom those believing would receive." I would estimate that 85% to 90% of all false teaching that springs from some portion of the Bible can be demonstrated to be false by a careful study of the surrounding verse or verses (the context) under consideration.*

- *Try to discover the exact meaning of each word, and the proper grammatical connection.*

- *As nearly as you can, consider all the passages in the Bible that shed light on the subject under study.[15]*

- *Never interpret a clear statement by an unclear statement. Always interpret the unclear in light of the clear one. Example: In Acts 16, the Philippian jailer who was on the verge of committing suicide, asked the following question: "Sirs, what must I do* to be saved?" Paul and Silas replied, "Believe on the Lord Jesus Christ and you will be saved" (verse 31). This is a clear statement on the subject of how to be saved. What God says plainly in one place He will not contradict elsewhere. For instance, when Paul said in Acts 27:31, "Unless these men stay in the ship, you cannot be saved," he was not referring to the salvation of their souls. He was referring to being saved or delivered from drowning, not about going to Heaven. God always says what He means and always means what He says, but we sometimes are much too careless in observing just what it is He does say.

- Try to avoid all personal prejudice and be honest in your use of Scripture.[16] Do not force the Word of God to support your theory. Do not interpret Scripture by your experience, but interpret all experiences in the light of Scripture. One of the major causes of false doctrine is a subjective approach to God's Word; that is, making the Bible fit one's experience or the experiences of others. Seek to discover what the Bible says and teaches, then judge every experience and theory—both yours and those of others—in light of the Word of God. If any theory or experience does not harmonize with God's Word, reject it as being unscriptural in nature. It may be very real and yet still *not be Scripturally based.*

● *Do not hurry your interpretation, especially of difficult passages.*

If you faithfully apply these principles to your own personal study of the Bible you will learn so much and the Scriptures will begin opening up to you; they will make sense in a very real, practical and life-changing way. A good simple rule of thumb for studying the Bible is to—

Read it.
Study it.
Believe it.
Act upon it.
Pass it on.

Appendix B

Verses Showing Belief Is Required for Salvation

Luke
7:48–50, 8:12, 18:42

John
1:7, 1:12, 2:23, 3:15–16, 3:18, 3:36, 4:39, 4:41–42, 5:24, 5:45–47, 6:29, 6:35, 6:40, 6:47, 7:38–39, 8:24, 8:29–30, 9:35–38, 10:24–26, 11:15, 11:25–26, 11:41–42, 12:36, 12:46, 13:19, 14:1, 17:20–21, 19:35, 20:29, 20:31

Acts
3:16, 4:4, 4:32, 8:12, 8:37, 9:42, 10:43, 10:45, 11:17, 11:21, 13:12, 13:39, 14:1, 14:23, 14:27, 15:7, 15:9, 16:31, 17:4–5, 17:11–12, 18:8, 18:27, 19:4, 20:21, 21:25, 26:18

Romans
1:16–17, 3:22, 3:25–28, 3:30, 4:3, 4:5, 4:9, 4:11, 4:13, 4:16, 4:23–24, 5:1–2, 9:30, 9:32–33, 10:4, 10:6, 10:8–10, 11:20, 11:30–32, 15:13

1 Corinthians
1:21

2 Corinthians
4:4

Galatians
2:16, 2:20, 3:2, 3:5–9, 3:11, 3:14, 3:22, 3:24, 3:26, 5:5

Ephesians
1:13, 1:19, 2:8, 3:17

Philippians
1:29, 3:9

1 Thessalonians
1:7, 2:10, 4:14

2 Thessalonians
1:10, 2:12–13, 3:2

1 Timothy
1:16, 3:16, 4:3, 4:10

2 Timothy
1:12, 3:15

Hebrews
4:2–3, 6:12, 10:39, 11:6–7, 31

James
2:23

1 Peter
1:5, 1:9, 1:21, 2:6–7

1 John
5:1, 5:5, 5:10, 5:13

Jude
1:5

Appendix C

The Story of a Man Named Dot

I first heard of Dot in the summer of 1969 when I was in northern Minnesota for a week of meetings. This is what I learned.

When Dot was born, his mother had wanted a daughter so badly that she named him Dorothy, and from infancy she let his hair grow long and dressed him as she would a little girl. She even sent him to school dressed as a girl. As a result he was often made fun of as a young child. Sometimes he would wear shorts under his skirt and when he got out of sight of the house he would take off the skirt and put it in a bush until he returned home from school later that day. This was very difficult for Dot and he became confused about his real place in life. He grew very suspicious—and later even afraid—of all women.

As is customary in that part of Minnesota, Dot became a lumberjack when he got older. But he always maintained that fear of women. He lived alone. In fact, he was so much of a loner in adulthood that rumors began to spread about him being somewhat weird and a hermit. Some even said he ate little girls. Few people ever did anything positive to try to discover why Dot behaved the way he did, or why he preferred to live alone.

When I arrived upon the scene that summer there was a group of mostly young couples who were new believers in Christ. They really seemed hungry to know more of God's Word.

The second day I was there, one of the men, Chan, briefly told me about Dot and asked if I'd be willing to go visit him. Chan and his wife had just recently trusted in Christ and were burdened for Dot. She would bake pies and the two of them would take them to Dot, and they would witness to him. In fact, they were the first ones to ever share the clear Gospel of God's grace to this lonely man. I was told that Dot lived in a little shack located on property that belonged to a church, and that he didn't like people to come around. But Chan assured me that if I wore my grubbiest clothes and went with him, Dot might let me talk to him. So, we planned to visit him the following afternoon.

The next day we drove to the lot where Dot's cabin was located. This "cabin" turned out to be a one-room shack no larger than 8–10 feet square. There was an old army folding cot, a couple of wooden crates and a lot of trash inside. He had lived in this shack for about 20 years. From the roadway we walked in knee-high grass for about 50 yards, and as we began to approach the shack Chan began to call for Dot. No one answered which puzzled Chan because normally he found Dot in the shack lying on his side on his rickety old cot.

As Chan continued to call we finally heard a reply from a pathway at the edge of the woods. It was Dot. We approached him and Chan assured him that I was a good friend who just wanted to have a word with him. I stood before a very old man who was bent with age, whose hands shook continuously, and who had a very blank, somewhat sad expression on his face. I didn't have to be told that this was a man who had known a great deal of personal sorrow in his life.

I shared the Gospel with Dot as we stood there on that path. As he listened he leaned heavily upon a piece of old board that he used for a cane. I especially emphasized that God loved him just the way he was. I told him how Christ came to die for sinners—that He loves sinners—and that if he would trust in this wonderful Savior, he would receive eternal life as God's free love-gift to him.

During most of my explanation of the Gospel, Dot just stared at the ground. When I got through—and he didn't respond—I reemphasized how God loved him just the way he was. I'll never forget his reply. He gave me a brief glance and said, "If that's true, then things sure have changed." I asked Dot, "When you say, 'things sure have changed' do you mean that you've always been told that you have to quit your sinning—your drinking, tobacco, cussing and wild living—and if you didn't, God wouldn't even consider saving you?" He uttered a simple, "Yep." I became very angry and replied, "Dot, I don't care what you've heard. The Bible says—and always has said—that God loves sinners and that Christ died for them." I again shared the love of God in sending His Son to be our Savior. And once more Dot simply stared at the ground, leaning on a board and a sturdy piece of a tree limb which he used as canes.

I went on and explained that although he had always heard that he had to stop his sinning before Christ would save him, the Bible says that "when we were still without strength" and "while we were still sinners, Christ died for the ungodly." I felt desperate; I so much longed for him to understand the true, free Gospel. I prayed earnestly for God to open his eyes. Finally, I said, "Look at me, Dot. Do you see the scar on my upper lip?" He looked and nodded that he did. I went on and said, "Well, Dot, the Bible says that when we get to Heaven we'll receive brand new bodies. So, when I get to Heaven I won't have any more scars on my body. And not only that, but the Bible also teaches that when we trust in Christ, He not only gives us eternal life right here and now, but when we get to Heaven God will give us a new name. Dot, if you will trust in Christ to save you, He will give you eternal life. And when you get to Heaven, He'll give you a brand new name. You will never again be called

Dorothy. You can trust in a God like that, can't you?" He thought a moment, still staring at the ground, and slowly nodded his head "yes." Once Dot understood that God's concern and love for him was this personal, it made that love very real to Dot. It helped open his eyes to the good news of the Gospel. The truth of the simple Gospel finally got through, and Dot indicated he was trusting in Christ alone for his salvation.

I put my hand on his shoulder, had a few more words of encouragement for him, and just before we left I asked him, "Dot, have you ever heard this before—what I've been telling you, that God loves you and Christ died to pay the complete penalty for all your sin; and that you could have eternal life just by trusting in Him?" He stared at the ground again, then replied, "No, not until Chan told me about it just the other day." I was wondering how long Dot had waited to hear the good news of the Gospel. Just before leaving I asked how many years young he was, and he said he thought he was 76.

I was driving that summer, speaking in various places. I arrived back home in late July or the early part of August. I wrote Dot a letter to thank him for letting me share the Gospel with him and reminding him of God's sure promise of eternal life. I sent the letter in care of Chan, knowing that Dot had no address and couldn't read. Later, I was told how Chan took the letter and read it to Dot. After reading it, he told Dot that he would take it and read to the folks at church and then bring it back to Dot. But Dot would have none of that. He told Chan that he had never received a letter before and didn't want this one out of his sight. I was told that a few days later Chan went by to see his new brother in Christ. Dot had brought in two long thorns from the woods and had tacked the letter to the wall at the foot of his bed. He said, "Every morning when I wake up, I look at that letter and thank God for sending a man all the way from Florida to tell me how to go to Heaven." All of this took place in July 1969. Dot passed away less than two months later. I'll never forget the lessons I learned from my brief encounter with this man.

Think on this: Dot was a man who lived in a so-called Christian community all his life, and was not only ignored by that community but shunned by it; he was someone who lived on church property for over 20 years and never heard the Gospel during that entire time; he was a man who had to live for 76 years before hearing about God's wonderful way of salvation for the first time—and that by a fairly new convert, Chan.

You may not know a "Dot," but perhaps in your neighborhood, in your apartment complex, or at your school there is someone whom others shun; they're not quite "with it." Perhaps they are considered odd, or at best, different. But don't forget, they are loved as much by God as anyone else, including you. They are precious in His sight. If you know

Christ as your Savior, perhaps you should share Him with them.

I think if genuine believers in Christ had grasped and lived in the light of the true Gospel over the years, we could have avoided many of the problems we've had to face. As children many of us sang, "Red, and yellow, black, and white; they are precious in His sight"—but all too often our lives show we do not really mean the words we sing. We pick and choose the people we'll witness to—we decide which kind of people are worthy of our time, our effort, and our brilliance. What a tragedy!

There may be someone in your life you have been avoiding or simply tolerating. Why not begin praying for them? Ask the Lord to give you His burden and love for them. Begin where you are—at your work, your school, your neighborhood—to reach others. Start today, and perhaps begin with those whom others may ignore—as Chan did with Dot.

Notes

1. For a complete list of these verses, see Appendix B.

2. See Psalm 5:4, Habakkuk 1:13, and Revelation 21:27.

3. See Isaiah 64:6; Jeremiah 17:9; Romans 3:10, 3:23, 8:7–8; and Ecclesiastes 7:20.

4. See Romans 6:23, Ezekiel 18:20, and Hebrews 9:27.

5. See Isaiah 53:6; 2 Corinthians 5:21; Philippians 3:9; 1 Peter 2:24, 3:18; Romans 1:3–4, 1:16–17; and 1 John 2:2.

6. See Romans 5:15–18, 6:23; Ephesians 2:8–9; and 2 Timothy 1:9.

7. See John 3:18, 3:36, 6:28–29, 6:47, 20:31; and Romans 4:5, and 9:30–10:4.

8. See John 5:24, 6:37, 6:39, 10:28–30; Romans 8:38–39; and 1 John 5:9–13.

9. See Philippians 1:29, 1 Thessalonians 3:3, and 1 Peter 2:19–22.

10. See Matthew 28:18–20; 1 Thessalonians 4:3, 5:18; and all

other commands He has given His children.

11. See Romans 12:38; 1 Corinthians 12:4–31; Ephesians 4:7, 4:11–16; and 1 Peter 4:10.

12. See John 7:37–39, 14:16–18; Acts 1:8; and Ephesians 4:30, and 5:18.

13. I also ask these two questions concerning the same statement made in Matthew 24:13, and I come to virtually the same conclusions.

14. See Ephesians 2:8–9 and Romans 4:5.

15. See 2 Peter 1:20 and 1 Corinthians 2:13.

16. See 2 Corinthians 4:2.

Scripture Index